AWAKEN

TO THE

MOMENT

— A KINGDOM REALITY —

BY

DR. RUSS MOYER

Published by:

McDougal & Associates
18896 Greenwell Springs Road
Greenwell Springs, LA 70739
www.thepublishedword.com

McDougal & Associates is an organization dedicated to the spreading of the Gospel of the Lord Jesus Christ to as many people as possible in the shortest time possible.

ISBN: 978-1-950398-79-9

Printed on demand in the U.S., the U.K., Australia and the EAU
For Worldwide Distribution

Presented To:

_____

By:

_____

On:

_____

Message:

_____

_____

_____

_____

Endorsements

Awaken to the Moment is a powerful reminder to live in the present NOW and embrace the supernatural opportunities that surround us every day. Russ Moyer's insightful and prophetic words, along with his powerful testimonies, encourage us to recognize the Spirit's direction, take notice of divine connections, and appreciate the beauty and wonder of God's glory all around us. This book is a must-read for anyone seeking to deepen their spiritual journey and live a more fulfilling and meaningful life with higher purpose. Highly recommended!

Joshua Mills
Bestselling author and minister, Power Portals
International Glory Ministries
www.joshuamills.com

◊

I've had the privilege of working with Dr. Russ Moyer several times now, and his message and word are always fresh and strategic, with a sharp prophetic edge. Like all of his other material, this book will help anyone see the bigger picture in God and define how " we must awaken to and fully understand the purpose of the Lord in this NOW moment." The time is now. Let's all *Awaken to the Moment!*

Randy King
Yorkton, Saskatchewan
Director, Full Gospel Business Men's Fellowship In Canada

◊

Awaken to the Moment is a book with a Kingdom vision from the heart of God. It will awaken and motivate you to press in for more. It will set your heart on fire with a passion to pursue the Kingdom reality that the Church is embarking upon—to rule and reign as kings and priests with authority and power in the presence of God, fulfilling the mandate of being the Bride of Christ, a holy habitation, God's remnant. We were born for such a time as this.

Dr. Russ Moyer is an apostolic, prophetic teacher and leader, a spiritual father and mentor whom I have known and walked in covenant with for more than twenty years now. His insight into the Kingdom will excite you and awaken you to a new hungry, passionate walk in the Spirit. You can hear the cry of the Spirit as Dr. Russ pours out the Father's heart for His

Church to awaken and partner with Him, to bring revival and restoration to His people.

This book is full of hope, faith, and expectations for the *Ecclesia*, the Bride of Christ, to walk in a new dimension of Kingdom reality. Now is the season to break out of traditional Sunday church, to be awakened and empowered, to experience the presence, power, and authority of God.

This book is a must-read for all, and I know you will be transformed by it. It will help you to understand what the Spirit is doing and saying to the Church today and encourage you to keep moving forward in the Kingdom reality.

Pastor Carol McLean
Jehovah Jireh Christian Ministries
Caledon, Ontario

◊

Awaken to the Moment: A Kingdom Reality is an incredible discourse on this prophetic moment in which we find ourselves. Dr. Russ Moyer has done an outstanding job of bringing both spiritual insight and inspiration to us for this journey. If you want a manual that will help you fully engage in revival, fulfill your call, and step into your revival destiny, this book is for you. If you embrace both the revelation and the practical principles laid out in this text, you will not only see transformation in your own life; you will become an agent of transformation. From the heart of a prophet, this is an Elijah Cry in the Spirit, and the cry is for you to *Awaken to the Moment* and manifest the power and presence of God. There is an anointing on this resource, and for those with ears to hear, this book is life-changing!

Pastor Patty Wallace
Vice President of Operations, Eagle Worldwide Ministries
Pastor, Transformation Centre, Hamilton, Ontario

◊

In his new book, Dr. Russ Moyer has a pulse on the times that we are living in. He is able to distinguish between a historical church mentality with a Kingdom Now view. You will not want to miss this revelation on the "Awakening" that is meant for this season with the new "Church" arising. I commend Dr. Russ on his most recent book, bringing a new view of where we are and where we are heading in the days before Jesus returns. You can be a part of these exciting days of seeing the harvest brought in by reading and doing what he expounds.

Apostle Gale Sheehan
Director Christian International
Apostolic Network

◊

Reading books can be a form of entertainment, but reading heartfelt letters from a mature prophet can potentially provoke a prophetic awakening in the reader. This book will undoubtedly lead you to an understanding of the prophetic landscape we have been experiencing and will continue to experience as the Church of Jesus. God is prophetic in His nature, and opening our eyes to the reality of His Kingdom allows us to be more effective in the areas of influence within our society.

Truly, as the Body of Christ, we need to demonstrate the power of His Holy Spirit without fear of criticism or attacks from minds that have philosophized about the Word but it has not been revealed to them. We are entering a moment of awakening, and we must understand the prophetic plans with which the Church must begin to build and restore.

This book will bring freedom to your life, as well as the assurance of moving in the direction to which the Spirit is calling us today. You hold a great treasure in your hands. Don't squander it, for it is God's wisdom for His people.

> *You are rising like the perfectly fitted stones of the temple; and your lives are being built up together upon the ideal foundation laid by the apostles and prophets, and best of all, you are connected to the Head Cornerstone of the building, the Anointed One, Jesus Christ himself!*
>
> Ephesians 2:20, TPT

Daniel Piedra Soto

Dedication

I dedicate this book *Awaken To the Moment: A Kingdom Reality* to the remnant that is coming out of the Bride, this generation that is marked by God with destiny and with an Elijah Cry on your hearts to prepare the way that will usher in the greatest harvest in history and the Second Coming of Christ!

> *Arise, shine;*
> *For your light has come!*
> *And the glory of the LORD is risen upon you.*
> *For behold, the darkness shall cover the earth,*
> *And deep darkness the people;*
> *But the Lord will arise over you,*
> *And His glory will be seen upon you.*
> *The Gentiles shall come to your light,*
> *And kings to the brightness of your rising.*
>
> *Lift up your eyes all around, and see:*
> *They all gather together, they come to you;*
> *Your sons shall come from afar,*
> *And your daughters shall be nursed at your side.*

Then you shall see and become radiant,
And your heart shall swell with joy;
Because the abundance of the sea shall be turned
to you,
The wealth of the Gentiles shall come to you.

Isaiah 60:1-5

Acknowledgments

I would like to acknowledge my wonderful wife, Mave Moyer. She is my soulmate, partner in ministry, and the love of my life. Mave is one of the most supportive, encouraging, kind, and loving people I've ever been around. I am truly blessed that God brought this precious gift my way, and I am also blessed that she is willing to live life on the prophetic edge with me.

I would also like to acknowledge Ashley Almas, our administrative assistant, along with our staff and team at The Dwelling Place of Pensacola and Eagle Worldwide Ministries in the U.S. and Canada.

Content

Foreword by Ward Simpson

I first met Dr. Russ Moyer in Pensacola, Florida during the Brownsville Revival, where the fires of revival were burning bright and hot, and where night after night, supernatural transformation took place in hearts and lives from around the world. Russ and I were privileged to be a part of this move of God and saw first-hand how this revival touched the world, ourselves included. Oh, how we enjoyed those years of soaking in God's presence and witnessing His Spirit touching people in front of our very eyes! Repentance was the message, righteousness the cry, and living a sold-out life for Jesus the result. Our lives will never be the same again, and we are eternally grateful to God for allowing us to be right there in the middle of it.

Awaken to the Moment

Since those days, Russ continues to do great things for God. He is a revivalist at heart, a man of God, called of God, and Lydia and I count it a joy to consider him and his dear wife, Mave, our friends and fellow co-laborers in Christ. He is a teacher, pastor, prophet, apostle, and evangelist, and his love for people, commitment to Christ, and passion for God's presence is immensely evident in every facet of his being.

This book is a prophetic call to get repositioned and realigned to the "now" plans and purposes of God. The Lord is at work and is refreshing, reviving, and restoring His Church in order to bring about societal transformation. Hell is raging, but the Kingdom of God is marching right along. Satan is spewing fear, depression, deception, grief, and all forms of trauma, but the King is at work, bringing salvation, deliverance, peace, provision, power, and victory. Because of this, Russ is making a clarion call to every believer to "awaken" and seize the moment, ensuring that we do not get lost and misguided between the Kingdom of God and the kingdoms of this world.

As children of God, we are citizens of His Kingdom and, therefore, require Kingdom vision and Kingdom understanding. We must be faithful, obedient, and submitted to Christ, the King, making Him our first priority and our pure passion. Our job is to preach the Good News, the Gospel of Jesus Christ, to the last, the least, and the lost, to be a light to the world, a good testimony and witness, and to live as model citizens of God's Kingdom in the fear of the Lord. Too many believers are getting caught up and or distracted with other "good" causes and forgetting the main goal of sharing the Good News. This is the moment of magnitude that we now encounter during these last days, and God wants to use you right where you are.

Sadly, the state of much of the population today is simply "going through the motions of life," with no real purpose in mind except to make it through another day. Additionally, there are others who crave riches and fame and are obsessed with material things. Like a drug, these are never satisfying, and those who depend on them, therefore, cannot wait for their next fix. This is the world we live in, and this is the world that God has given us to reach with the Good News of Jesus Christ. This is our mission field, and the answer is not found in politics, social services, sports, or entertainment, but can only be found in the Gospel of the Kingdom. This is the prophetic cry of this book, a cry for Kingdom reality, the greater, bigger picture of the greater glory that is to come. It is a call to action, a call for us to once again turn to God, a call to *Awaken to the Moment*!

As we consider and pray about this pro-phetic call, let us remember that this Christian life we live is described in the Bible as a "race." It is a long-distance marathon that requires discipline, humility, perseverance, dedication, training, stamina, faith, and focus. This race is not a sprint, a gallop, or a jog in the park, but rather a race that we must run, all the while keeping our focus on the prize of eternal life and glory. We were born to run, raised to run and God has equipped us to run with gifts, tal-ents, and a supernatural mantle or anointing. Like Elisha, who served Elijah, we, too, can be servants of the King. Don't let the current political, social, or economic landscape deter you because God has a Kingdom plan and purpose for your life and wants to use you right where you are. Whether you are at school, at work or at play, God is at work throughout the Earth and desires to work through you.

Take Elisha as an example: He received his mantle during the ruthless and evil reign of Jezebel and at a time when his predecessor was being hunted and persecuted. What was Elisha doing in spite of the gloom and doom? He was hard at work ploughing the field, and God saw something in Elisha that attracted Him. He saw a faithful and diligent servant working in spite of everything going on around him. Elisha answered the Awaken-to-the-Moment call and followed Elijah immediately, but he would first have to become a servant before he could become a leader (a Kingdom principle). It took Moses forty years. Joseph endured trials, betrayals, slavery, and prison. David, for many years, had the title of king but no throne. And Jesus set the ultimate example and also came as a servant. As in the days of Elijah and

Awaken to the Moment

Elisha, the world is filled with evil, and, as in the days of Elijah and Elisha, God is looking for His people who are faithful and diligent servants and are willing to stay the course. Will you answer the call? This is one of the greatest hours in the history of mankind, and you and I get to live it. This is the season for a great harvest. This is the time for spiritual repositioning and realignment. It's time to *Awaken to the Moment*!

Ward Simpson
President GOD TV

Repent therefore and be converted, that your sins may be blotted out, so that times of refreshing may come from the presence of the Lord, and that He may send Jesus Christ, who was preached to you before, whom heaven must receive until the times of restoration of all things, which God has spoken by the mouth of all His holy prophets since the world began.
— Acts 3:19-21

Introduction

As I was writing this book, *Awaken to the Moment: A Kingdom Reality*, I hosted an online Elijah Cry for the International Coalition of Prophetic Leaders. We gathered a group of mature prophetic leaders for an online forum. We host these prophetic forums periodically with different prophets, leaders, and prophetic voices because each of us in the prophetic community only hears in part. We need one another to see the bigger picture in God and to fellowship, work, and walk together as a prophetic community.

I'm excited by the response. So many people are beginning to turn in the right direction for revelation, wisdom, and understanding. We have just stepped over the threshold of a great awakening that has already begun. There is an Elijah Cry on the heart of God in this moment!

Awaken to the Moment

Yes, we are called to prepare the way for the great end-time move of the Spirit and to declare boldly the Second Coming of Christ. However, the deeper cry on the heart of God is this: "Where are My Elijahs in this generation?" He is calling us forth, to turn again to Him, His purpose and plan for this prophetic and strategic moment in time, not just the issues and conditions we are confronted with now— politically, economically, and culturally—but rather this Kingdom moment. This is a cry for Kingdom reality, the greater, bigger picture of the greater glory that is to come.

Most of the other things that are happening to us and around us are signs of the times and attacks meant to divide and distract us from the true purpose of God, which is to declare His dominion, His coming, and His victory. We must believe for an opening of our spiritual ears to hear, as the seventh angel sounds the trumpet and proclaims the Kingdom:

> *Then the seventh angel sounded: And there were loud voices in heaven, saying, "The kingdoms of this world have become the kingdoms of our*

Lord and of His Christ, and He shall reign forever and ever!" Revelation 11:15

We must awaken to and fully understand the purpose of the Lord in this NOW moment. He is refreshing, reviving, and restoring His Church to bring a major transformation to our society.

We have just completed a great season of transition, one the most difficult seasons in the history of the Church. The aftereffects are still with us and will continue throughout the coming months. We keep wanting to hear that we will wake up tomorrow, and it's all over, or it's the way things used to be, but the truth is that it will continue to get worse before it gets better—a lot worse. Then, however, it will get better than we could ever imagine.

Personally, I believe that the best is yet to come. The greatest days of the Church are ahead of us, not behind us. We are moving toward the tipping point, but we are just not there quite yet.

End-time prophecy is being fulfilled before our eyes. The battle of good and evil is raging and intensifying. Jesus described it perfectly in Matthew 24:3-31:

Awaken to the Moment

Now, as He sat on the Mount of Olives, the disciples came to Him privately, saying, "Tell us, when will these things be? And what will be the sign of Your coming, and of the end of the age?" And Jesus answered and said to them: "Take heed that no one deceives you. For many will come in My name, saying, 'I am the Christ,' and will deceive many. And you will hear of wars and rumors of wars. See that you are not troubled; for all these things must come to pass, but the end is not yet. For nation will rise against nation, and kingdom against kingdom. And there will be famines, pestilences, and earthquakes in various places. All these are the beginning of sorrows.

"Then they will deliver you up to tribulation and kill you, and you will be hated by all nations for My name's sake. And then many will be offended, will betray one another, and will hate one another. Then many false prophets will rise up and deceive many. And because lawlessness will abound, the love of many will grow cold. But he who endures to the end shall be saved. And this gospel of the kingdom will be preached in all the world as a witness to all the nations, and then the end will come.

"Therefore when you see the 'abomination of desolation,' spoken of by Daniel the prophet, standing in the holy place" (whoever reads, let him understand), "then let those who are in Judea flee to the mountains. Let him who is on the housetop not go down to take anything out of his house. And let him who is in the field not go back to get his clothes. But woe to those who are pregnant and to those who are nursing babies in those days! And pray that your flight may not be in winter or on the Sabbath. For then there will be great tribulation, such as has not been since the beginning of the world until this time, no, nor ever shall be. And unless those days were shortened, no flesh would be saved; but for the elect's sake those days will be shortened.

"Then if anyone says to you, 'Look, here is the Christ!' or 'There!' do not believe it. For false christs and false prophets will rise and show great signs and wonders to deceive, if possible, even the elect. See, I have told you beforehand.

"Therefore if they say to you, 'Look, He is in the desert!' do not go out; or 'Look, He is in the inner rooms!' do not believe it. For as the lightning comes from the east and flashes to the

west, so also will the coming of the Son of Man be. For wherever the carcass is, there the eagles will be gathered together.

"Immediately after the tribulation of those days the sun will be darkened, and the moon will not give its light; the stars will fall from heaven, and the powers of the heavens will be shaken. Then the sign of the Son of Man will appear in heaven, and then all the tribes of the earth will mourn, and they will see the Son of Man coming on the clouds of heaven with power and great glory. And He will send His angels with a great sound of a trumpet, and they will gather together His elect from the four winds, from one end of heaven to the other."

Paul spoke of this apostasy in 1 Timothy 4:1-5:

Now the Spirit expressly says that in latter times some will depart from the faith, giving heed to deceiving spirits and doctrines of demons, speaking lies in hypocrisy, having their own conscience seared with a hot iron, forbidding to marry, and commanding to abstain from foods which God created to be received with thanksgiving by those who believe and know the truth. For

*every creature of God is good, and nothing is to
be refused if it is received with thanksgiving; for
it is sanctified by the word of God and prayer.*

Paul also accurately described this moment
in 2 Timothy 3:1-9:

*But know this, that in the last days perilous
times will come: For men will be lovers of
themselves, lovers of money, boasters, proud,
blasphemers, disobedient to parents, unthankful, unholy, unloving, unforgiving, slanderers,
without self-control, brutal, despisers of good,
traitors, headstrong, haughty, lovers of pleasure rather than lovers of God, having a form
of godliness but denying its power. And from
such people turn away! For of this sort are those
who creep into households and make captives
of gullible women loaded down with sins, led
away by various lusts, always learning and
never able to come to the knowledge of the truth.
Now as Jannes and Jambres resisted Moses, so
do these also resist the truth: men of corrupt
minds, disapproved concerning the faith; but
they will progress no further, for their folly will
be manifest to all, as theirs also was.*

Awaken to the Moment

The sheep and goat nations are aligning in an effort to bring a new world order. There is chaos, anarchy, confusion, lawlessness, and moral decay facing North America and also an apostasy, a falling away from Christ and His Church. Violence is rampant in our homes, on our streets, and our nations, men calling good evil and evil good, wars and rumors of wars. At the same time, we are experiencing the beginning stages of a turnaround and are seeing glimpses of God's glory, but the Church is a big ship, and it takes time to turn it. In the meantime, many are left living in deception, denial, and depression.

Sadly, at times, we have allowed the enemy to turn us into critics, attacking one another with accusations, judgements, and curses. Still, I firmly believe that we are in the season of the restoration of all things. As Peter preached on the Day of Pentecost:

> *Repent therefore and be converted, that your sins may be blotted out, so that times of refreshing may come from the presence of the Lord, and that He may send Jesus Christ, who was preached to you before, whom heaven must*

receive until the times of restoration of all things, which God has spoken by the mouth of all His holy prophets since the world began.
Acts 3:19-21

I'm a dual citizen of the United States and Canada, two of the greatest nations in the free world. However, even here we are experiencing major issues in every area of our society. Globally, we are facing attacks from the outside, from the changing one-world order. Illegal immigrants are storming our borders, bringing violence, crime, drugs, and human trafficking into our countries. At the same time, we are being attacked from the inside with division, disunity, political chaos, violence in our homes, in our schools, and on our streets. Politicians, the media, and secular voices are even alluding to the chaos of this moment.

On the other hand, the entertainment industry is now producing quality full-length movies on the Jesus Movement and other powerful spiritual movements. The scene is set for the fulfillment of end-time prophecy and for the restoration of all things. This includes the coming Tribulation and the Second Coming of Christ.

Awaken to the Moment

Changes in politics, business, education, and culture will not, in and of themselves, make restoration happen. We need Jesus to show up with a move of His Spirit, the Third and final Reformation.

My objective for this book is to give you a prophetic perspective of the strategic and prophetic moment we are in and the season that lies ahead so that you are properly positioned and aligned. Now is the time, and we must *Awaken to the Moment*. This is a *Kingdom Reality*!

—Russ Moyer
President of Eagle Worldwide Ministries
US and Canada

CHANGES IN POLITICS, BUSINESS, EDUCATION, AND CULTURE WILL NOT, IN AND OF THEMSELVES, MAKE RESTORATION HAPPEN. WE NEED JESUS TO SHOW UP WITH A MOVE OF HIS SPIRIT, THE THIRD AND FINAL REFORMATION!

Chapter 1

Beyond a Great Kingdom Reset!

But seek ye first the kingdom of God, and his righteousness; and all these things shall be added unto you. Matthew 6:33, KJV

These last few years have been challenging, to say the least, and everyone is talking about a Kingdom reset. For more than thirty years now the apostolic and prophetic community has been prophesying, emphasizing, and teaching a Kingdom message and Kingdom culture. We, the Church, have been going through one of the most dramatic and radical seasons of change, transition, and transformation in Church history, to bring us to where we are NOW.

The game is this: The prophet and pastor of one church says, "Here is God." Another says,

"No, God is there." Maybe that's where He was, but this is where He is now. Why? Because He is almost always on the move. Every time we step into the river of God, we step into a new place in that river. Even if I were to step in at the same spot on the bank where I stepped into the river before, it's a new place, for the river is moving. Yes, God is the same yesterday, today, and forever, but He is doing a new thing and singing a new song. There is also a generation that has been patiently waiting for the real, and I want to announce: It's reality time. NOW is the time.

We have loved the stories of the Azusa Street Revival, the Welsh Revival, the Jesus Movement, the Charismatic Movement, the Latter Rain, the Toronto Blessing, the Pensacola Outpouring, and others, but that won't do anymore. We need a fresh touch of Heaven. We must manifest what we have been speaking, preaching, and teaching, and that is Kingdom reality. We can't just say, "Yes, Lord, we see and hear what You want" and then purpose to build something different than what He has told us. We've all paid a price to come out of Egypt (church mentality) to the apostolic structure on this journey, and we don't want to go back to the old way or stop short and perish in the wilderness. Our determined goal is to press on until we have reached the Promised Land.

As God moves, we must move too. As we get deeper and deeper into this end-time battle, we must not just speak change and Kingdom but manifest it in the reality of the moment in each of our lives.

I want to assure you: we are on the right path, and this is the heart of God for us. I also want to let you know that the reality of it will not be easy for us to embrace. Why? Because it will require change from us and a new mindset. We must challenge our old church traditions, culture, and mindsets.

Jesus came preaching the Gospel of the Kingdom, and it challenged the Jewish religious establishment of His day to change from an exclusive to an inclusive vision. They suddenly had to open the ranks of the chosen people to everyone because of the grafting in of the gentiles. In Acts 10, we find the story of Pater preaching at the household of Cornelius, a Roman. To do this, God had to call Peter to take a fresh look at what He calls "clean" or "unclean."

Awaken to the Moment

Jesus demonstrated this new attitude in His teachings and began with:

> *From that time Jesus began to preach, and to say, Repent: for the kingdom of heaven is at hand.* Matthew 4:17, KJV

Men and women had strayed from God and were following their own thoughts, but Isaiah declared:

> *For my thoughts are not your thoughts, neither are your ways my ways, saith the LORD. For as the heavens are higher than the earth, so are my ways higher than your ways, and my thoughts than your thoughts. For as the rain cometh down, and the snow from heaven, and returneth not thither, but watereth the earth, and maketh it bring forth and bud, that it may give seed to the sower, and bread to the eater: so shall my word be that goeth forth out of my mouth: it shall not return unto me void, but it shall accomplish that which I please, and it shall prosper in the thing whereto I sent it.*
> Isaiah 55:8-13, KJV

God's thoughts are so much higher than our own. He stays the same, but we must change. We must change and continue to change. It is not enough to allow change, we must embrace change, fall in love with it.

You and I must learn Kingdom principles, the Kingdom mindset, the Kingdom government structure, and Kingdom covenant to bring us to a full reality, seeing ourselves as a work in progress on a journey and not as having arrived in any sense of the word.

The very first principle of the Kingdom is this: in a kingdom, the king rules, not the people. The laws the king institutes are non-negotiable. This is the reason Jesus taught first things first, when He said we should *"seek first the Kingdom of God and His righteousness"* (Matthew 6:33.) You and I need a fresh understanding of the Kingdom, its origin, its purpose, and its principles.

The Kingdom speaks of dominion:

> *And God said, Let us make man in our image, after our likeness: and let them have dominion over the fish of the sea, and over the fowl of the air, and over the cattle, and over all the earth, and over every creeping thing that creepeth*

upon the earth. So God created man in his own image, in the image of God created he him; male and female created he them. And God blessed them, and God said unto them, Be fruitful, and multiply, and replenish the earth, and subdue it: and have dominion over the fish of the sea, and over the fowl of the air, and over every living thing that moveth upon the earth.

Genesis 1:26-28, KJV

God gave man an inherent delegated authority to have dominion over the earth. He was to rule and reign, being master over a designated territory. We know the story of how the first Adam lost this dominion, but we also know the story of how Jesus, the Second Adam, regained it. The Scriptures declare that it is God's pleasure to give us the Kingdom:

Fear not, little flock; for it is your Father's good pleasure to give you the kingdom.

Luke 12:32, KJV

Because God is our Father, in this Kingdom He wants us to establish sons, not subjects. As children of God, we are even members of the

Royal Family, and the Kingdom is our inheritance. Just think of the pleasure God gets by bestowing His blessings on His children. He delights in sharing His Kingdom with us.

While it is true that we must suffer some in the process of claiming this Kingdom, it will surely be worth it all. Paul wrote:

> *For I reckon that the sufferings of this present time are not worthy to be compared with the glory which shall be revealed in us. For the earnest expectation of the creature waiteth for the manifestation of the sons of God.*
>
> Romans 8:18-19, KJV

Another principle of the Kingdom is that we must have Kingdom vision, seeing through the eyes of the King, to make it work as it should.

When Jesus came, He preached the Kingdom, and He made us citizens of the Kingdom, not just members of a religion. Our purpose is to extend the Kingdom rule and reign here on Earth. Leaders in the Kingdom today must train to reign.

Another important principle of the Kingdom concerns finances. It all belongs to the King, and

He requires a lot more of us than a tithe. He is calling for Kingdom stewardship. This includes covenant Kingdom businesses and marketplace ministries, with a mission focused on the mandate of Christ in the Earth today.

All of our resources must be going to further the Kingdom. Everything in our lives must be focused on seeding the Kingdom. This requires our time, our energy, our efforts, our attention, and our creativity. No, it's not all about money. We are to give a lot more than money. We are to give ourselves to the King and His Kingdom.

God has appointed us as His ambassadors, and therefore we must think and act like the King. We must ask ourselves, "What would Jesus think in this situation?" and "What would Jesus do in this situation?" That's why we need the mind of Christ. When we have it, it will broaden our view, expand our vision, and remove all lack and limits from the equation. Why? Because we know who our Daddy is and what He owns. He owns it all.

At the same time we are ambassadors, we are sons and daughters. Who could better represent the King than His own loving children?

Therefore if any man be in Christ, he is a new creature: old things are passed away; behold, all things are become new. And all things are of God, who hath reconciled us to himself by Jesus Christ, and hath given to us the ministry of reconciliation; to wit, that God was in Christ, reconciling the world unto himself, not imputing their trespasses unto them; and hath committed unto us the word of reconciliation. Now then we are ambassadors for Christ, as though God did beseech you by us: we pray you in Christ's stead, be ye reconciled to God.

2 Corinthians 5:17-20, KJV

Yes, Jesus preached the Gospel of the Kingdom in word, and He also demonstrated it in deed:

And Jesus went about all the cities and villages, teaching in their synagogues, and preaching the gospel of the kingdom, and healing every sickness and every disease among the people.

Matthew 9:35, KJV

From that time Jesus began to preach, and to say, Repent: for the kingdom of heaven is at hand.

Matthew 4:17, KJV

Awaken to the Moment

This was Jesus' first public declaration after leaving Nazareth:

> *Now when Jesus had heard that John was cast into prison, he departed into Galilee; and leaving Nazareth, he came and dwelt in Capernaum, which is upon the sea coast, in the borders of Zabulon and Nephthalim: that it might be fulfilled which was spoken by Esaias the prophet, saying, The land of Zabulon, and the land of Nephthalim, by the way of the sea, beyond Jordan, Galilee of the Gentiles; the people which sat in darkness saw great light; and to them which sat in the region and shadow of death light is sprung up. From that time Jesus began to preach and to say, Repent, for the kingdom of heaven is at hand.* Matthew 4:12-17, KJV

So, our mission is: *"Repent for the Kingdom of heaven is at hand."* This involves turning to God and His way of thinking. Kingdom vision, whether we are talking local, domestic, or foreign missions, focuses on the harvest. This Kingdom principle will even determine when time as we know it will end:

And Jesus answered and said unto them, Take heed that no man deceive you. For many shall come in my name, saying, I am Christ; and shall deceive many. And ye shall hear of wars and rumours of wars: see that ye be not troubled: for all these things must come to pass, but the end is not yet. For nation shall rise against nation, and kingdom against kingdom: and there shall be famines, and pestilences, and earthquakes, in divers places. All these are the beginning of sorrows.

Then shall they deliver you up to be afflicted, and shall kill you: and ye shall be hated of all nations for my name's sake. And then shall many be offended, and shall betray one another, and shall hate one another. And many false prophets shall rise, and shall deceive many. And because iniquity shall abound, the love of many shall wax cold. But he that shall endure unto the end, the same shall be saved. And this gospel of the kingdom shall be preached in all the world for a witness unto all nations; and then shall the end come.　　　Matthew 24:4-14, KJV

As we make the turn toward the Kingdom reset, it's Kingdom reality. We must refresh, revive, restore, pursue, and recover all! Paul wrote to the Ephesian believers:

> *Therefore I also, after I heard of your faith in the Lord Jesus and your love for all the saints, do not cease to give thanks for you, making mention of you in my prayers: that the God of our Lord Jesus Christ, the Father of glory, may give to you the spirit of wisdom and revelation in the knowledge of Him, the eyes of your understanding being enlightened; that you may know what is the hope of His calling, what are the riches of the glory of His inheritance in the saints, and what is the exceeding greatness of His power toward us who believe, according to the working of His mighty power which He worked in Christ when He raised Him from the dead and seated Him at His right hand in the heavenly places, far above all principality and power and might and dominion, and every name that is named, not only in this age but also in that which is to come.*
>
> Ephesians 1:15-21

You and I must awaken, and we must *Awaken to the Moment*! This is the *Kingdom Reality.*

PRAYER:

My prayer today, for all of us in His Church, is this:

Lord, let us each find our way, our place, our Kingdom purpose. Grant us, oh Lord, that Kingdom vision that would allow us to see beyond ourselves. Open the eyes of our understanding, that we may see things through the eyes Your heart, that we may focus on You and Your Kingdom first and foremost. Let us see things through the eyes of the King of Glory. May we not get caught between the two worlds, the two visions, the two opinions. Help us to reset our priority order and look at the bigger picture and the greater glory that is to come.

In Jesus' glorious name!

THE VERY FIRST PRINCIPLE OF THE KINGDOM IS THIS: IN A KINGDOM, THE KING RULES, NOT THE PEOPLE. THE LAWS THE KING INSTITUTES ARE NON-NEGOTIABLE!

Chapter 2

The Essence and Importance of the Gospel of the Kingdom

In those days John the Baptist came preaching in the wilderness of Judea, and saying, "Repent, for the kingdom of heaven is at hand!" For this is he who was spoken of by the prophet Isaiah, saying: "The voice of one crying in the wilderness: 'Prepare the way of the LORD; Make His paths straight.' "

Now John himself was clothed in camel's hair, with a leather belt around his waist; and his food was locusts and wild honey. Then Jerusalem, all Judea, and all the region around the Jordan went out to him and were baptized by him in the Jordan, confessing their sins.

Awaken to the Moment

But when he saw many of the Pharisees and Sadducees coming to his baptism, he said to them, "Brood of vipers! Who warned you to flee from the wrath to come? Therefore bear fruits worthy of repentance, and do not think to say to yourselves, 'We have Abraham as our father.' For I say to you that God is able to raise up children to Abraham from these stones. And even now the ax is laid to the root of the trees. Therefore every tree which does not bear good fruit is cut down and thrown into the fire. I indeed baptize you with water unto repentance, but He who is coming after me is mightier than I, whose sandals I am not worthy to carry. He will baptize you with the Holy Spirit and fire. His winnowing fan is in His hand, and He will thoroughly clean out His threshing floor, and gather His wheat into the barn; but He will burn up the chaff with unquenchable fire." Matthew 3:1-12

Yes, there is a 911 Elijah Cry on the heart of God in this season, and the cry of His heart is: "Where are My Elijahs in this generation?" Jesus spoke so accurately of this end-time moment when His disciples asked Him what the sign of His coming would be. He said:

Take heed that no man deceive you.

Matthew 24:4, KJV

What does this warning represent? It represents the sign of the times and the end of the age. The entire passage is worth reading:

> *Now as He sat on the Mount of Olives, the disciples came to Him privately, saying, "Tell us, when will these things be? And what will be the sign of Your coming, and of the end of the age?" And Jesus answered and said to them: "Take heed that no one deceives you. For many will come in My name, saying, 'I am the Christ,' and will deceive many. And you will hear of wars and rumors of wars. See that you are not troubled; for all these things must come to pass, but the end is not yet. For nation will rise against nation, and kingdom against kingdom. And there will be famines, pestilences, and earthquakes in various places. All these are the beginning of sorrows.*
> *"Then they will deliver you up to tribulation and kill you, and you will be hated by all nations for My name's sake. And then many will be offended, will betray one another, and will hate*

53

one another. Then many false prophets will rise up and deceive many. And because lawlessness will abound, the love of many will grow cold. But he who endures to the end shall be saved. And this gospel of the kingdom will be preached in all the world as a witness to all the nations, and then the end will come."

Matthew 24:3-14

Next, Jesus spoke of the Great Tribulation and the Second Coming of Christ:

For then there will be great tribulation, such as has not been since the beginning of the world until this time, no, nor ever shall be. And unless those days were shortened, no flesh would be saved; but for the elect's sake those days will be shortened.
"Then if anyone says to you, 'Look, here is the Christ!' or 'There!' do not believe it. For false christs and false prophets will rise and show great signs and wonders to deceive, if possible, even the elect. See, I have told you beforehand."

Matthew 24:21-25

It is harvest time, but many will be deceived by false prophets and good ideas conceived by the media and man. My wife, Mave, has said, "An unsanctified imagination brings perverted revelation," and it's true.

I believe firmly in the Seven Mountain Mandate concept and strategy. It suggests that seven centers of influence must be reached. They are family, religion, education, media, entertainment, business, and government. However, the Seven Mountain Mandate is not the answer to our situation and the way home. The answer is also not found in politics, social services, sports, or entertainment. It can only be found in the Gospel of the Kingdom.

What is this gospel? It's not a prosperity gospel, not a political gospel, not a seeker-friendly gospel, and not a hyper-grace gospel. It is God's own brand of Gospel, and we need to focus on it more now than ever.

John the Baptist declared and preached it in his day:

> *In those days John the Baptist came preaching in the wilderness of Judea, and saying, "Repent, for the kingdom of heaven is at hand!" For this*

*is he who was spoken of by the prophet Isaiah,
saying:*
"The voice of one crying in the wilderness:
*'Prepare the way of the L*ORD*;*
Make His paths straight."   Matthew 3:1-3

Jesus preached this message in word and
demonstrated it in power. The miracles, signs,
and wonders that He and the early believers
performed glorified the God of Israel:

*Jesus departed from there, skirted the Sea of
Galilee, and went up on the mountain and sat
down there. Then great multitudes came to
Him, having with them the lame, blind, mute,
maimed, and many others; and they laid them
down at Jesus' feet, and He healed them. So the
multitude marveled when they saw the mute
speaking, the maimed made whole, the lame
walking, and the blind seeing; and they glorified
the God of Israel.*   Matthew 15:29-31

Phillip preached this Gospel and, because of
it, brought a great move of the Spirit to Samaria.
The Gospel of the Kingdom is the message of
salvation, proclaiming Christ, who was born,

crucified, and resurrected for the salvation of man from sin. When Philip the evangelist preached *"the good news of the kingdom of God,"* men and women believed and were baptized (Acts 8:12, NIV). His preaching was with demonstrations and power:

> *Then Philip went down to the city of Samaria and preached Christ to them. And the multitudes with one accord heeded the things spoken by Philip, hearing and seeing the miracles which he did. For unclean spirits, crying with a loud voice, came out of many who were possessed; and many who were paralyzed and lame were healed. And there was great joy in that city.* Acts 8:5-8

The Apostle Paul, who was a Pharisee of the Pharisees, also preached this Gospel, he said, in weakness, fear, and much trembling:

> *And I, brethren, when I came to you, did not come with excellence of speech or of wisdom declaring to you the testimony of God. For I determined not to know anything among you except Jesus Christ and Him crucified. I was with you in weakness, in fear, and in much*

57

trembling. And my speech and my preaching were not with persuasive words of human wisdom, but in demonstration of the Spirit and of power, that your faith should not be in the wisdom of men but in the power of God.

1 Corinthians 2:1-5

There is power in the Word. Some found God and trusted Him in the Old Testament, but many more in the New. He is the same yesterday, today, and forever. He is the God of the generations—the God of Abraham, Isaac, and Jacob, the God of Elijah who answered by fire and power. His name is Faithful and True. He was on time for Elijah, and He will surely be on time for you and me.

This God spoke through His prophets, kings, and priests of old, and He still honors faith today:

But without faith it is impossible to please Him, for he who comes to God must believe that He is, and that He is a rewarder of those who diligently seek Him. Hebrews 11:6

Isaiah found this God in the Temple. Jeremiah found Him too, and He brought

His people out of captivity. This God wants to be found:

> *I will be found by you, says the LORD, and I will bring you back from your captivity; I will gather you from all the nations and from all the places where I have driven you, says the LORD, and I will bring you to the place from which I cause you to be carried away captive.*
>
> *Because you have said, "The LORD has raised up prophets for us in Babylon" — therefore thus says the LORD concerning the king who sits on the throne of David, concerning all the people who dwell in this city, and concerning your brethren who have not gone out with you into captivity — thus says the LORD of hosts: Behold, I will send on them the sword, the famine, and the pestilence, and will make them like rotten figs that cannot be eaten, they are so bad. And I will pursue them with the sword, with famine, and with pestilence; and I will deliver them to trouble among all the kingdoms of the earth — to be a curse, an astonishment, a hissing, and a reproach among all the nations where I have driven them, because they have not heeded My words, says the LORD, which I sent to them by*

Awaken to the Moment

My servants the prophets, rising up early and sending them; neither would you heed, says the LORD. Therefore hear the word of the LORD, all you of the captivity, whom I have sent from Jerusalem to Babylon.

Thus says the LORD of hosts, the God of Israel, concerning Ahab the son of Kolaiah, and Zedekiah the son of Maaseiah, who prophesy a lie to you in My name: Behold, I will deliver them into the hand of Nebuchadnezzar king of Babylon, and he shall slay them before your eyes. And because of them a curse shall be taken up by all the captivity of Judah who are in Babylon, saying, "The LORD make you like Zedekiah and Ahab, whom the king of Babylon roasted in the fire"; because they have done disgraceful things in Israel, have committed adultery with their neighbors' wives, and have spoken lying words in My name, which I have not commanded them. Indeed I know, and am a witness, says the LORD.

You shall also speak to Shemaiah the Nehelamite, saying, Thus speaks the LORD of hosts, the God of Israel, saying: You have sent letters in your name to all the people who are at Jerusalem, to Zephaniah the son of Maaseiah the priest, and to all the priests, saying, "The LORD has made you priest instead of Jehoiada the priest, so that there should be officers in the house of the LORD over every man who is demented and considers himself a prophet, that you should put him in prison and in the stocks. Now therefore, why have you not rebuked Jeremiah of Anathoth who makes himself a prophet to you? For he has sent to us in Babylon, saying, 'This captivity is long; build houses and dwell in them, and plant gardens and eat their fruit.' "

Now Zephaniah the priest read this letter in the hearing of Jeremiah the prophet. Then the word of the LORD came to Jeremiah, saying: Send to all those in captivity, saying, Thus says the LORD concerning Shemaiah the Nehelamite: Because Shemaiah has prophesied to you, and I have not sent him, and he has caused you to trust in a lie—therefore thus says the LORD: Behold, I will punish Shemaiah the Nehelamite and his family: he shall not have anyone to dwell among this people, nor shall he see the good that I will do for My people, says the LORD, because he has taught rebellion against the LORD."

Jeremiah 29:14-32

Awaken to the Moment

I believe we each have as much of God as we want. How can I say that? Because His promise is that if we take a step toward Him, He will take a step toward us. Let us repent and turn again to God today. I declare this to be the acceptable year of the Lord, and the day of the vengeance of our God. Let us resolve to follow Him in the ministry of reconciliation, following in His footsteps, and press in to the Messiah Mandate anointing and the blessings of Isaiah 61:

> *The Spirit of the LORD God is upon Me,*
> *Because the LORD has anointed Me*
> *To preach good tidings to the poor;*
> *He has sent Me to heal the brokenhearted,*
> *To proclaim liberty to the captives,*
> *And the opening of the prison to those who are*
> *bound;*
> *To proclaim the acceptable year of the LORD,*
> *And the day of vengeance of our God;*
> *To comfort all who mourn,*
> *To console those who mourn in Zion,*
> *To give them beauty for ashes,*
> *The oil of joy for mourning,*
> *The garment of praise for the spirit of heaviness;*
> *That they may be called trees of righteousness,*

The planting of the LORD, *that He may be glorified.*

And they shall rebuild the old ruins,
They shall raise up the former desolations,
And they shall repair the ruined cities,
The desolations of many generations.
Strangers shall stand and feed your flocks,
And the sons of the foreigner
Shall be your plowmen and your vinedressers.
But you shall be named the priests of the LORD,
They shall call you the servants of our God.
You shall eat the riches of the Gentiles,
And in their glory you shall boast.
Instead of your shame you shall have double honor,
And instead of confusion they shall rejoice in their portion.
Therefore in their land they shall possess double;
Everlasting joy shall be theirs.
For I, the LORD, *love justice;*
I hate robbery for burnt offering;
I will direct their work in truth,
And will make with them an everlasting covenant.
Their descendants shall be known among the Gentiles,

63

Awaken to the Moment

And their offspring among the people.
All who see them shall acknowledge them,
That they are the posterity whom the LORD has blessed.

I will greatly rejoice in the LORD,
My soul shall be joyful in my God;
For He has clothed me with the garments of salvation,
He has covered me with the robe of righteousness,
As a bridegroom decks himself with ornaments,
And as a bride adorns herself with her jewels.
For as the earth brings forth its bud,
As the garden causes the things that are sown in it to spring forth,
So the LORD God will cause righteousness and praise to spring forth before all the nations."

Isaiah 61:1-11

Let us reason with the Lord, for He has a plan for your life. You are called and chosen. Let us purpose ourselves to be faithful in this prophetic and strategic moment in time. Let us be faithful and step up, step in, and step out in faith and faithfulness. We will see this scripture fulfilled, along with all the others in God's Word:

> *These will make war with the Lamb, and the Lamb will overcome them, for He is Lord of lords and King of kings; and those who are with Him are called, chosen, and faithful.*
>
> Revelation 17:14

Yes, you and I must awaken, and we must *Awaken to the Moment*! This is the *Kingdom Reality*.

PRAYER:

Heavenly Father, strengthen, support and work with us as we awaken to this strategic moment, that we may preach the Gospel of the Kingdom with demonstrations of Your power, the saving, healing, and life-changing Gospel of Jesus Christ. Help us to focus and no longer be distracted by the things of this world. Holy Spirit, lead us, guide us, direct us, and protect us, that we may bring glory and honor to Your name!

In Jesus' name,
Amen!

I BELIEVE WE EACH HAVE AS MUCH OF GOD AS WE WANT. HOW CAN I SAY THAT? BECAUSE HIS PROMISE IS THAT IF WE TAKE A STEP TOWARD HIM, HE WILL TAKE A STEP TOWARD US!

Chapter 3

The Rise of Revival Hubs

*And no one puts new wine into old wineskins;
or else the new wine bursts the wineskins, the
wine is spilled, and the wineskins are ruined.
But new wine must be put into new wineskins.*

Mark 2:22

What an incredible season we are living in! In this chapter, I want to give you some straight talk about revival. I also want to describe some models you can tell God has His hand on and is blessing in this new season.

The theme the Lord gave me for 2023 was Refresh, Revive, and Restore, and we are seeing this happening right now before our very eyes. What an incredible winter camp we had in the glory, the power, and presence of God!

And then we had our "Days of Awe," in which we had absolutely wonderful demonstrations of the Spirit, with profound prophetic words, healings, deliverances, baptisms in the Spirit, and times of radical Tabernacle worship and also of holy hush. The Lord is doing a very deep, intimate, and personal thing in the hearts of His people.

Revival is a personal thing, first and foremost. God is not a cookie-cutter God. Some people miss His best because they are expecting Him to do what He did or is doing somewhere else for somebody else. But God expresses Himself in many different ways, in many different individuals, in different cities, nations, and denominations. Don't get too distracted and caught up in what He is doing in someone else. It's what He is doing in YOU and what He wants to do in YOU that is important.

God has a perfect plan for you, and it will be different from what He is doing in others and even different than what you have experienced in the past. As noted earlier, each time you step into the river of God, you are always stepping into a "new place" in that river. There is fire and refreshing and revival in the river, but it may look different than in other places, other churches, and other individuals.

God anoints us personally and individually with creativity and understanding, and by His power and presence He challenges our faith and willingness to change. The Body of Christ is made up of so many different parts and pieces, all with a unique purpose and plan, and God aligns them in perfect positioning. However, there are special seasons and moments in each believer's life in which the Lord realigns us to prepare us for, or to facilitate, our assignment, in order to fulfill our destiny.

In these end days, the Spirit will visit every tribe, tongue, and nation. This is the beginning of that. Let Him continue to do His work of preparation in you. Don't get lost in someone else's thing or expression. It's all about you and God. As you yield to Him, He will challenge the stereotypes in your thinking and do a new thing in you. Here are some important thoughts to ponder in your honest pursuit of God:

1. Be careful you are not at the airport when your ship comes in. Sometimes we are running around looking everywhere else

at the very moment God is bringing something new our way.

2. Pursue the God of Revival, not the revivalist, or even revival itself. Revival is a
personal thing, and the revivalist is just a
human being. We are not chasing Elijah,
Steve Hill, Rodney Howard Brown, or any
other man or woman. We are pursuing the
God of Revival, and when we touch Him,
we will catch the fire that never goes out.

3. I am very hungry for a move of God but
remember: His first name is Holy. If something isn't holy, I don't want any part of it.

4. God can and will move in any expression
or manifestation that open and hungry
hearts are truly seeking and are willing to
receive. He will move in many denominations with signs, wonders, and miracles.
Let's give Him space and grace to do what
He wants to do.

5. Don't criticize and discount something
you don't understand. I hear people saying

with such certainty, "Oh, this is 'true revival'!" They are three weeks in and have become the new experts. Let's let God be God. He will do something unique and different in you in this season and in everyone who is open to this moment. Your keys and theirs are unique and different.

When I came to Pensacola in 1997, God gave me two revelations. First, in the prayer meetings that were led at the Bible school by Lila Terhune, I saw a figure that looked like Mickey Mouse. His feet were very big, and he was lifting them up and down very fast in a beautiful vat of honey. Gradually he began to move them slower and slower until he could not longer move at all. He was stuck in the honey.

Just then God said, "Many of My people, even those with the greatest calls, will get stuck in the honey and linger and not go to the harvest. In this way, they will settle for less than the best I have for them." Then God showed me intercessors coming out of the closet and moving to the forefront in His prophetic army. He said they would have to "get up off the floor and go to war."

Awaken to the Moment

After a great revival service, I was praying and thanking God for all He had done, and He said to me, "It isn't just about good meetings; it's about discipleship and mentoring and making sons and daughters who will follow in your footsteps and extend the Kingdom." He said that we needed to touch our roots to reach our destiny, that it was all generations walking and working together.

There are a few people who are called to labor in support roles at different hubs and centers. Most are called there to be refreshed, revived, restored, equipped, empowered, and launched into the harvest fields the Lord has prepared for them.

Revival needs to be pastored, but it must be done with an open hand and an open heart, allowing harvest workers and leaders to come and go. In each service, the manifest presence of God will seem to intensify. This is good. It is very good because God is always good, but it's going to get better as things around us get worse. The war between good and evil is raging in every city, every nation, every home, and in every heart. Our theme verse for the book bears repeating:

> *Repent therefore and be converted, that your sins may be blotted out, so that times of refreshing may come from the presence of the Lord, and that He may send Jesus Christ, who was preached to you before, whom heaven must receive until the times of restoration of all things, which God has spoken by the mouth of all His holy prophets since the world began.*
>
> Acts 3:19-21

A new wine skin is the end-time church model the Lord is raising up at this moment in time, the emerging Church.

Let's see if we can describe the model prophetically so we can see, believe, receive, and build with a blueprint strategy and structure that is on the heart of the Lord in this moment in time. We must not just awaken; we must awaken to the moment!

In their recent book, *Revival Hubs Rising*,[1] Ryan LeStrange and Jennifer LeClaire use terms like "revival hubs," "apostolic revival centres," "glory hubs," and "Kingdom centres" to describe the Church God is raising up. This confirms the new pattern the Lord

1. Amberely, New Zealand, Impact Awakening Ministries, Inc.: 2016

75

has established in many locations. It is, basically, a breaking of the mold of the traditional Sunday church. God is calling for a new wineskin to hold His new wine:

> *And no one puts new wine into old wineskins; or else the new wine bursts the wineskins, the wine is spilled, and the wineskins are ruined. But new wine must be put into new wineskins.*
>
> Mark 2:22

Verse 21 uses a different analogy, but it puts forth the same principle:

> *No one sews a piece of unshrunk cloth on an old garment; or else the new piece pulls away from the old, and the tear is made worse.*
>
> Mark 2:21

Paul wrote:

> *Though I am free and belong to no one, I have made myself a slave to everyone, to win as many as possible. To the Jews I became like a Jew, to win the Jews. To those under the law I became like one under the law (though I myself am not*

under the law), so as to win those under the law. To those not having the law I became like one not having the law (though I am not free from God's law but am under Christ's law), so as to win those not having the law. To the weak I became weak, to win the weak. I have become all things to all people so that by all possible means I might save some. I do all this for the sake of the gospel, that I may share in its blessings.

1 Corinthians 9:19-23, NIV

Here are some things you can look for and expect to see in these apostolic hubs and revival centers so that you can recognize, align with, believe and receive from them. These equipping and empowering centers will have some of these components, so we can recognize them:

1) At the core is **a healthy local church**. That doesn't mean a mega-church. It means a healthy church that's maturing and being equipped and empowered, a people being prepared and launched into their destiny.

77

2) **Healing rooms**, providing personal ministry, freedom ministry, deliverance, physical and inner healing!

3) **A school of the Spirit**, equipping the saints for practical ministry through teaching, impartation, and demonstration of the Spirit, the Word and the Spirit working together. There will be worship to God in Spirit and in truth and in the beauty of holiness.

4) **Practical ministry training**, living ministering and leading in the Spirit. In this season, it is at the speed of change and in the midst of chaos.

5) **A house of prayer**:

> *Even them I will bring to My holy mountain,*
> *And make them joyful in My house of prayer.*
> *Their burnt offerings and their sacrifices*
> *Will be accepted on My altar;*
> *For My house shall be called a house of prayer*
> *for all nations."*   Isaiah 56:7

This is what Jesus said about His Father's house in Mark 11:17:

And he taught, saying unto them, Is it not written, My house shall be called of all nations the house of prayer? but ye have made it a den of thieves. (KJV)

What should we expect in His house? The power of prayer and intercession, prophetic petition and warfare, a war room, throne room praise and worship, declaration and proclamation, the prayer of faith, healing through calling for the elders, the laying on of hands for the sick, and a strong burden for unity (see John 17).

6) **A house of worship**:

> *After this I will return, and will build again the tabernacle of David, which is fallen down; and I will build again the ruins thereof, and I will set it up.*   Acts 15:16, KJV

7) **A house led by the Spirit**:

> *For as many as are led by the Spirit of God, these are the sons of God.*   Romans 8:14

8) **A house of discipleship and mentoring**:

For the earnest expectation of the creature waiteth for the manifestation of the sons of God.
Romans 8:19, KJV

9) **The raising up of sons and daughters**, not slaves and servants, but sons and daughters with a servant's heart, raising them up for service both in the nuclear, extended, and para-church families. Most of the miracles of the early church and the ministry of Christ were outside the four walls of the church, out in the marketplace.

10) **A house of healing.**

11) **A house of hope.**

12) **A house of restoration and reconciliation:** We are all called to the ministry of reconciliation, and the Messiah mandate is also our mandate. We must follow in Jesus' footsteps:

And He is before all things, and in Him all things consist. And He is the head of the body, the church, who is the beginning, the firstborn from the dead, that in all things He may have the preeminence. For it pleased the Father that in Him all the fullness should dwell, and by Him to reconcile all things to Himself, by Him, whether things on earth or things in heaven, having made peace through the blood of His cross. And you, who once were alienated and enemies in your mind by wicked works, yet now He has reconciled in the body of His flesh through death, to present you holy, and blameless, and above reproach in His sight— if indeed you continue in the faith, grounded and steadfast, and are not moved away from the hope of the gospel which you heard, which was preached to every creature under heaven, of which I, Paul, became a minister.

Colossians 1:17-23

13) **A house for the outcast, the down and out, and the up and out:**

The LORD doth build up Jerusalem: he gathereth together the outcasts of Israel.

Psalm 147:2, KJV

14) **A house for all nations**, one new man, neither Greek nor Jew, neither man or woman, from every stream flowing together, bringing down the man-made barriers that separate from every tribe, tongue, and nation, letting go of the old man and pressing into the new creation realty of who we are in Christ and who Christ is in us, *"the Hope of Glory."*

15) **A house of radical tabernacle worship.** Paul declared it to the Jerusalem Council:

> *And with this the words of the prophets agree, just as it is written: "After this I will return And will rebuild the tabernacle of David, which has fallen down; I will rebuild its ruins, and I will set it up; so that the rest of mankind may seek the Lord, even all the Gentiles who are called by My name, says the Lord who does all these things."* Acts 15:15-17

Yes, you and I must awaken, and we must *Awaken to the Moment*! This is the *Kingdom Reality.*

Prayer:

My prayer for those of us who are trail-blazers and pioneers, the torchbearers of our generation:

Jesus, let us see, recognize, and decree in this season the places, platforms, patterns, and models You are creating. Let us properly connect with, align with, and receive from those You have chosen to use. Thank You for where and how You are moving. I ask that You would send revival to our homes, churches, communities, and nations, that You would set our hearts ablaze, and that You would teach us be torchbearers for You wherever we go, bringing new life and new hope, and that You would bear fruit in us, to us, and through us, and fruit that lasts.

In Jesus' glorious name.

REVIVAL IS A PERSONAL THING, FIRST AND FOREMOST. SOME PEOPLE MISS GOD'S BEST BECAUSE THEY ARE EXPECTING HIM TO DO WHAT HE DID OR IS DOING SOMEWHERE ELSE FOR SOMEBODY ELSE!

Chapter 4

Our Own Journey in the Miraculous Realm

No one sews a piece of unshrunk cloth on an old garment; or else the new piece pulls away from the old, and the tear is made worse.

Mark 2:21

I began to describe prophetically this transformation we are now experiencing in my dissertation and later turned it into a book entitled *Can These Bones Live?*. In the pages of that book, I spoke about the restoration of the end-time Church. For more than fifteen years now, I have been referring to these apostolic resource centers as revival hubs and revival centers and have described what they are to look like in general.

Awaken to the Moment

As a New Testament Church, we are to raise up a governing model of fivefold firefight teams. That was part of the original vision/mission statement that God gave me in 2000 to birth Eagle Worldwide Ministries. That first revelation came in a dream, and then God confirmed it with a prophetic word given in Vineland, New Jersey, and another word from Christian International. The Lord is going to refresh, revive, and restore His Church!

These revival centers are to be apostolically led and prophetically influenced. They will be apostolic resource centers and revival hubs and will be rising up in many different places across the country and around the world.

In 1998, I received a word from a prophet in Kentucky, where we were doing a prophetic conference, about a wagon wheel in the mud. It created a rut. I was the wagon wheel, and I was stuck in Pensacola in revival, but I was called to the nations.

In 1999, Paul Lackey and Gale Sheehan, two mature prophets at Christian International, prophesied about sitting around a campfire and sending teams to the nations and the ministry of restoration and reconciliation of the human family and the family of God. I was given by God a name and mission statement, and I wrote it down before there ever was a ministry called Eagle Worldwide Ministries. This mission statement included all of what we would do long before we knew we would do it.

In 2001, I led a team of ten to do a revival conference at Chestnut Assembly in Vineland, New Jersey. The pastor there was a wonderful man of God, hungry for a move of the Spirit. During our team prayer time, one of the men began to prophesy over us that he saw a wagon wheel with twelve spokes and that we would be at the hub. The spokes would be fivefold apostolic firefight teams going out to the nations. He spoke to me about hubs, centers, and wagon wheels, which prophetically speaks of pioneering works, and the number 12 is the number for the apostolic.

When we left there, I was going back to our home and office in Copetown, Ontario. Only a few days after our trip, I drove past a sign on Highway 52 about two or three miles from my home. It had a wagon wheel on it, and it said: "Welcome to Copetown, the Hub of the Universe." I stopped by the side of the road, got out of my car, and started thanking God for that sign.

I counted the spokes on the wagon wheel carefully and then began to repent and praise God louder. There were twelve. I had received the word but had not totally believed it. Now I was kneeling on the roadside, crying out to God.

God then spoke to me in an audible voice, "Your promise is right across the street." I looked, and there was a closed-down, over-grown campground. I called Mave at the office and told her what had happened, and she came right down, and we prayed together.

We walked over to the property and saw a man clearing some land. I asked him if it was for sale. He said that he and his wife had just purchased it, and they had a big vision for a senior retirement village and park. I told him I was a missionary and would like to buy it, but he answered, "We're not interested in selling."

Then the man asked me, "Where are you a missionary to?"

I said, "Here in Canada and other nations."

He laughed and said, "Why does Canada need missionaries?"

I said, "Because most of the people here are not born-again believers and have no relationship with the Lord."

I asked him if it was okay for us to come there and walk and pray on the property, and he answered, "Sure! Anytime!"

We started bringing prayer teams there to pray and declare the word of the Lord over the property. I told my wife that first day that I felt the Lord had told me the city would not give the man permission to build what he wanted. If the proper zoning could not be obtained, then he might be happy to sell us the land.

Lo and behold, eight months later the Lord woke me one morning and said, "Today is the day to call him." I called the man and asked how the project was moving along. He told me the city was causing a lot of trouble, and there were many delays and fees. I said, "We're still interested in talking about buying it. Why don't you and your wife stop over for a coffee."

"Yes," he said, "we'll come. My wife actually had a dream about the property last night."

"Oh," I said, "I also had a dream."

They came over, and we talked awhile, and the wife shared her dream. She had seen many different people on the property, missionaries were there with the flags of the nations, and she saw family campfires burning. I went into the other room and brought her our Vision Statement and the plans we had for the property God had given us dreams and visions about. She began to weep, and so did I.

I said, "Your dream is just like my dream. You and I both heard God Himself tell us in dreams what He wants to do with your property. If you and your husband want to persevere with your plans, then Mave and I will stop what we're doing and help you. But if you're not able to carry out your plan, then sell us the property, and we will fulfill the vision."

They agreed, and we sat down and drew up an agreement to purchase the land for $600,00.00. We didn't have anything close to the required twenty percent down payment. We had only a few hundred dollars in the bank, but within three or four months the money had come in, and the financing was approved. This provision was an amazing miracle because I wasn't yet a Canadian citizen, and I had no steady job or income.

That day, when they were visiting, Mave and I agreed and signed the papers. Then, when the other couple had left and we were still standing on the porch, Mave said to me, "Where are we going to get that kind of money?"

I said, "I believe this revelation is from God, and He will supply. I'm not going to worry about finances."

For the next twenty years we put up buildings, held summer camp using tents, and worshiped God with people from many nations. We held special events where many miracles and memories were made. So many lives were changed and transformed on that property, all for the glory of God!

We have pioneered, visited and partnered with other revival hubs and apostolic centers in Aurora, Ontario, Hamilton, Ontario, and Toronto, Ontario, Quebec City, Pensacola, Florida and a number of other places and nations.

The New Testament government, laid out in Ephesians 14:11-12, is a fully functioning, five-fold ministry in operation:

> *And He Himself gave some to be apostles, some prophets, some evangelists, and some pastors and teachers, for the equipping of the saints for*

*the work of ministry, for the edifying of the body
of Christ.*   Ephesians 4:11-12

The Lord clearly describes the Church in
Ephesians 2:19-22 as a spiritual house, His
"dwelling place," built on the foundation of apostles and prophets, the Chief Cornerstone being
Christ Himself. Any builder will tell you that a
cornerstone is the first stone laid on a foundation, and its purpose is to bring structure and
alignment to all the other stones. They must all
be aligned with that stone. This requires prophets and apostles walking and working together,
aligning with Christ and His principles and
teachings—the foundation of our faith.

I have been on the Advisory Board for
many years for the International Coalition
of Apostolic Leaders. Eight years ago I pioneered the International Coalition of Prophetic
Leaders, to gather prophetic voices and walk
in unity with the apostolic community. This is
critical. God has a plan:

> *Now, therefore, you are no longer strangers and
> foreigners, but fellow citizens with the saints
> and members of the household of God, having*

been built on the foundation of the apostles and prophets, Jesus Christ Himself being the chief cornerstone, in whom the whole building, being fitted together, grows into a holy temple in the Lord, in whom you also are being built together for a dwelling place of God in the Spirit.

Ephesians 2:19-22

We are building the House of God and the Army of God together. We are birthing and building together with a blueprint and a heavenly plan.

Yes, you and I must awaken, and we must *Awaken to the Moment*! This is the *Kingdom Reality.*

PRAYER:

I come to You, Father, in the name of Jesus Christ and in the power of the Holy Spirit. Thank You that You are the God of signs, wonders, and miracles and that You are the same yesterday, today, and forever. Anoint us afresh today and confirm Your Word with signs following. I declare a release of fresh fire over Your people. Let us manifest Your glory and move with ease into the supernatural realm, flowing in the gifts of the Spirit, demonstrating Your great love.

Amen!

REVIVAL NEEDS TO BE PASTORED, BUT IT MUST BE DONE WITH AN OPEN HAND AND AN OPEN HEART!

Chapter 5

The Needed Fear of the Lord

The fear of the LORD is the instruction of wisdom; and before honour is humility.
                    Proverbs 15:33, KJV

The NIV says it this way:

Wisdom's instruction is to fear the LORD, and humility comes before honor. Proverbs 15:33, NIV

The fear of the LORD is the beginning of wisdom: and the knowledge of the Holy One is understanding.   Proverbs 9:10, KJV

We need many things in this hour, but one of the greatest needs is a restoration of the fear of God. Think of it! The fear of the Lord is the beginning of wisdom. That's a biggie, but the fear of the Lord is so much more. There are great promises and benefits connected to having the fear of the Lord.

Psalm 103 opens with these words:

> *Bless the LORD, O my soul;*
> *And all that is within me, bless His holy name!*
> *Bless the LORD, O my soul,*
> *And forget not all His benefits:*
> *Who forgives all your iniquities,*
> *Who heals all your diseases,*
> *Who redeems your life from destruction,*
> *Who crowns you with lovingkindness and tender mercies,*
> *Who satisfies your mouth with good things,*
> *So that your youth is renewed like the eagle's.*
>   Psalm 103:1-5

These are all wonderful reasons to pursue and cultivate a healthy fear of the Lord. A lack of fear of the Lord is one of the reasons sin is so rampant in the Church today and why many people "act out."

America needs revival, the Church of Jesus Christ needs revival. What we need to experience true revival is a revival of the fear of the Lord. I'm not talking about being afraid of God; I'm talking about a healthy fear of the Lord, a reverence for God.

It seems that in church settings today, the most important thing is for the pastor to be cool. He has to look cool in his high-heeled designer sneakers. He has to act cool, and He has to throw in some good jokes. Worship today has to be fun. Let's not get too serious about things. If we get too serious, we might become stiff, serious, intense (or, God forbid), "religious."

Is it any wonder that our churches are shallow and superficial in their walk? We seem to be immune from Holy Spirit conviction, and, as a result, far too many people are living compromised lives. We don't need to be afraid of God, but we do need to recognize who He is and that we live our lives in His presence, and therefore, should be doing things that are pleasing in His sight. Yes, how we act matters to God.

Every one of us should be in awe of God:

> *The fear of the LORD is to hate evil;*
> *Pride, and arrogancy, and the evil way*
> *And the perverse mouth I hate.* Proverbs 8:13, KJV

Awaken to the Moment

Unfortunately, today, the church at large wants to be completely free of the fear of the Lord, as they enjoy living out the latest and brightest revelation. We have provided flashy new carts to carry God's presence, when it should be carried on the shoulders of priests who love, honor, and reverence Him. His Word declares:

> *See that ye refuse not him that speaketh. For if they escaped not who refused him that spake on earth, much more shall not we escape, if we turn away from him that speaketh from heaven: whose voice then shook the earth: but now he hath promised, saying, Yet once more I shake not the earth only, but also heaven. And this word, Yet once more, signifieth the removing of those things that are shaken, as of things that are made, that those things which cannot be shaken may remain. Wherefore we receiving a kingdom which cannot be moved, let us have grace, whereby we may serve God acceptably with reverence and godly fear: for our God is a consuming fire.*
>
> Hebrews 12:25-29, KJV

> *For the Lord thy God is a consuming fire, even a jealous God.* Deuteronomy 4:24, KJV

Duncan Campbell, the great revivalist in the Hebrides, said, "Man needs to be found prostrate on the ground and flee to Christ for refuge."[1] When Steve Hill, during the Pensacola Revival of the late 1990s, brought forth an urgent cry for holiness and deep heartfelt repentance, it was a wake-up call I needed to lay down my life, pick up my cross, and follow Christ. I thank God for Steve Hill. He had a healthy fear of God and was able to share that urgency with many thousands of believers from around the world.

Like most things in the Spirit, we believers are now caught between two places: the world view (a pattern of happy life and carnal success) and our hunger and thirst for the deeper things of God that can only be found in the fear of the Lord and the awe of His presence. We have a choice to make. We must *Awaken to the Moment*. It is time to let God be God. This is a *Kingdom Reality*.

---

1. From a sermon on YouTube

Prayer:

Heavenly Father, we need a healthy fear of the Lord today like never before. May we reverence You in everything we do. Remove from us the fear of man and give us wisdom to fear You and You alone, that we would not bow our knee to the idols of this world or to men, but to You and You alone, that we would worship You in Spirit and truth, and that everything we do and say would bring glory and honor to Your name, that we would not seek fortune and fame, but Your heart, Your face in humility, so that we may access Your grace to run and win our race, fulfill our destinies and leave a legacy for You. You are worthy of all glory, all honor, and all praise.

In Jesus' name,
amen!

AMERICA NEEDS REVIVAL, THE CHURCH OF JESUS CHRIST NEEDS REVIVAL, AND WHAT WE NEED TO EXPERIENCE TRUE REVIVAL IS A REVIVAL OF THE FEAR OF THE LORD, A HEALTHY REVERENCE FOR GOD!

Chapter 6

Healing the Traumas We Have Suffered While Waiting

The Spirit of the Lord God is upon Me,
Because the Lord has anointed Me
To preach good tidings to the poor;
He has sent Me to heal the brokenhearted,
To proclaim liberty to the captives,
And the opening of the prison to those who are
bound;
To proclaim the acceptable year of the Lord,
And the day of vengeance of our God;
To comfort all who mourn,
To console those who mourn in Zion,
To give them beauty for ashes,
The oil of joy for mourning,
The garment of praise for the spirit of heaviness;
That they may be called trees of righteousness,

Awaken to the Moment

The planting of the LORD, that He may be glorified.
And they shall rebuild the old ruins,
They shall raise up the former desolations,
And they shall repair the ruined cities,
The desolations of many generations.

Isaiah 61:1-4

This season is the prelude to the greatest move of the Spirit in all of history. Christ's earthly ministry was one of reconciliation, and when He returned to Heaven, He gave that ministry to us. As ambassadors of Christ, we now have the same mandate as the Messiah.

This mandate was confirmed in Matthew 10 when Jesus sent out the twelve apostles and again in Mark 16:15-20, when He spoke to all believers on the day of His ascension. We are to preach the Gospel of the Kingdom, lay hands on the sick, cast out demons in His name, bind up the brokenhearted, and declare the acceptable day of the Lord. What are we waiting for?

God said through the prophet Hosea:

My people are destroyed for lack of knowledge.
Because you have rejected knowledge,

I also will reject you from being priest for Me;
Because you have forgotten the law of your God,
I also will forget your children. Hosea 4:6

There are five spirits that most of us are experiencing that are opposing the end-time Church right now in this post-pandemic season. They are:

1). Fear
2). Depression
3). Deception
4). Grief
5). Trauma

Each of these are attacking our faith, bringing confusion and frustration, and causing many of us in the Body of Christ to lose our way.

David was the greatest king Israel ever had, and he was a worship warrior. He was quick to go to war and quick to go to the throne of God in prayer. He sang:

He maketh my feet like hinds' feet,
And setteth me upon my high places.

Awaken to the Moment

He teacheth my hands to war,
So that a bow of steel is broken by mine arms."

Psalm 18:33-34, KJV

Paul exhorted us:

> *Finally, my brethren, be strong in the Lord,*
> *and in the power of his might. Put on the whole*
> *armour of God, that ye may be able to stand*
> *against the wiles of the devil. For we wrestle*
> *not against flesh and blood, but against prin-*
> *cipalities, against powers, against the rulers*
> *of the darkness of this world, against spiritual*
> *wickedness in high places.*

Ephesians 6:10-12, KJV

Praise and worship are the highest forms of warfare. Our weapons are not carnal, but spiritual.

Most of us, after all the battles we've gone through these last few years, are suffering from trauma, fear, grief, depression, and deception. These spirits are causing havoc in the Church, and, combined with government restrictions, have brought on and added to the great falling away or the apostasy foretold in the sacred

Scriptures. We need to close the door on trauma and the resulting PTSD (Post-Traumatic Stress Disorder).

Do Christians suffer PTSD? They do. The Lord gave me a dream about soldiers in battle and showed me that I and many others, particularly leaders and spiritual warriors in the Body of Christ, were suffering from PTSD. This PTSD has to end. Today is a day of freedom, a day of liberty, and where the Spirit of the Lord is there is liberty:

> *Nevertheless when it shall turn to the Lord, the veil shall be taken away. Now the Lord is that Spirit: and where the Spirit of the Lord is, there is liberty. But we all, with open face beholding as in a glass the glory of the Lord, are changed into the same image from glory to glory, even as by the Spirit of Lord.*
>
> 2 Corinthians 3:16-18, KJV

As we have seen, Isaiah foretold:

> *The Spirit of the Lord God is upon me; because the Lord hath anointed me to preach good tidings unto the meek; he hath sent me to bind up*

*the brokenhearted, to proclaim liberty to the
captives, and the opening of the prison to them
that are bound.*　　　　　　　Isaiah 61:1, KJV

The Lord showed me that just as PTSD occurs in the natural realm, it also occurs in the spiritual realm. How does it affect us? It affects us physically, mentally, emotionally, and spiritually. God also showed me that there are triggers we need to be aware of that can open the door for this enemy to come back and revisit us.

What is PTSD? PTSD has been defined as "a condition of persistent mental and emotional stress occurring as a result of injury or severe psychological shock, typically involving the disturbance of sleep and the constant, vivid recall of the experience, with dulled responses to others and to the outside world."[1] God said:

*And he shall speak great words against the most
High, and shall wear out the saints of the most
High, and think to change times and laws: and
they shall be given into his hand until a time
and times and the dividing of time.*
　　　　　　　　　　　　Daniel 7:25, KJV

---

1. https://www.oxfordreference.com/

In the aftermath of World War II, this malady, suffered by many soldiers in that war, was widely known as Battle Fatigue. It is a psychological disorder that develops in some individuals who have had major traumatic experiences (for example, have been in a serious accident or through the ravages of war). The person affected by PTSD is typically numb at first. Later, they experience many other symptoms. These include: depression, excessive irritability, guilt (for having survived while others died), recurrent nightmares, flashbacks to the traumatic scene, and overreaction to sudden noises.

PTSD or Post-Traumatic Stress Disorder became known as such in the 1970s due to the adjustment problems many Vietnam veterans suffered back home. Think of it: many veterans of war end up as drug addicts, alcoholics, and homeless. This should not be, but that is the reality.

Who is susceptible to or likely to suffer from PTSD? Here is a partial list:

- Soldiers in combat situations and suffering from battle fatigue

- People who are involved in any kind of accident and other traumatic event, even including public scandal, betrayal, bankruptcy, or incarceration
- People who have been diagnosed with and treated for serious illnesses and diseases
- People encountering near-death situations
- People who suffer third-party trauma—first responders, caregivers, family members, loved ones who, through relationship, suffer

Some of the most common symptoms of PTSD include the following:

- Intense feelings of distress when reminded of a tragic event
- Extreme physical reaction to reminders of trauma, such as nausea, sweating, or a pounding heart
- Invasive, upsetting memories of a tragedy
- Flashbacks (feeling like the trauma is happening again)
- Nightmares of either frightening things or of the event
- Loss of interest in life and daily activities

- Feeling emotionally numb and detached from other people
- A sense of not leading a normal life (not having a positive outlook on the future)
- Avoiding certain activities, feelings, thoughts, or places that remind you of the tragedy
- Difficulty remembering important aspects of a tragic event

Some common reactions to PTSD include:

1. Detachment from Others

One of the first symptoms of post-traumatic stress disorder is detachment from others. This can happen for a myriad of complicated reasons. Often, those with PTSD are afraid of how they might behave in front of others. They worry that they might become angry or react strangely to normal occurrences.

2. Flashbacks

Flashbacks are another symptom of PTSD. This causes a person to relive a traumatic event. The emotional response is different for everyone; however, flashbacks often cause feelings of panic, extreme stress, and physical issues like fainting, heart palpitations, and high blood pressure.

3. Nightmares

Frequent nightmares are a common symptom of PTSD. These nightmares may focus on the event that created the trauma or they may appear unrelated. Nightmares are different from flashbacks in that they occur on a subconscious level during sleep, while flashbacks take place while the mind is alert and awake.

4. Avoiding Reminders

Someone with PTSD may avoid situations that remind them of the events surrounding the trauma. For example, if the traumatic event happened at work, then the person with PTSD may have difficulty returning to their job. Additionally, they may not want to be around family or friends they associate with the traumatic event. This symptom can interfere with one's livelihood and/or social life.

5. Insomnia

Insomnia, or the inability to sleep, is another symptom of PTSD. There are many reasons insomnia occurs. Some people may find that they keep worrying about the event that caused the trauma, making it difficult to clear their minds and drift off to sleep. The knowledge that nightmares begin after they drift off can also make sleep difficult. Doctors can prescribe medications or holistic methods to help reduce instances of this debilitating symptom. Too often, sufferers turn to alcohol and drugs.

What is the answer? Jesus came that we might have life and life more abundant. His mandate (and ours) is to bring healing and hope. We need to learn to fight with the spiritual weapons God has given us. What are they?

- The power and the presence of God
- The blood of Christ
- The cross
- Declaration and confirmation
- The power of prayer
- The Word of God
- The name of Jesus

When we have a need, we must confess our weakness, our need, our shortcomings, one to another and pray for one another. There is no shame in having a need. We all do. Call on the elders of the church to come and anoint you and pray the prayer of faith over you. God's promise is: *"the prayer of faith will save the sick, and the Lord will raise him up"* (James 5:15, KJV). God also promised:

> *The yoke shall be destroyed because of the anointing.* Isaiah 10:27b, KJV

> *"Not by might nor by power, but by My Spirit," Says the Lord of hosts.* Zechariah 4:6

And, again, let us remember the words of Isaiah:

> *The Spirit of the Lord God is upon me; because the Lord hath anointed me to preach good tidings unto the meek; he hath sent me to bind up the brokenhearted, to proclaim liberty to the captives, and the opening of the prison to them that are bound.* Isaiah 61:1, KJV

Yes, we must *Awaken to the Moment*, for there is healing for every trauma. This is a *Kingdom Reality*.

PRAYER:

In Your name, Jesus Christ, I plead the blood of Jesus over us now, over our minds, bodies, and emotions. I bind every tormenting and harassing spirit that has been released against us in this past season. I bind the spirits of trauma, pain, depression, distraction, disappointment, mourning, and grief. I command them, in the name of Jesus Christ, to loose their hold on every one of us and leave us now in Jesus' name. I take authority over you now and command you to leave and go to the place Jesus says to go. I declare liberty and freedom, healing and hope, in Jesus' name. Father, let Your love fill every hurt and any empty place in us now.

In Jesus' mighty and glorious name.

THIS SEASON IS THE PRELUDE TO THE GREATEST MOVE OF THE SPIRIT IN ALL OF HISTORY!

Chapter 7

Reclaiming All Power
and All Authority

*The thief does not come except to steal, and to
kill, and to destroy. I have come that they may
have life, and that they may have it more abundantly.* John 10:10

The thief has his agenda, and he attends to it
well. We, however, as instruments of God, have
our own agenda, and it is very different. We know
the will of our God and King, and He has given
us all power and all authority to see it happen:

*And Jesus came and spoke to them, saying, "All
authority has been given to Me in heaven and
on earth. Go therefore and make disciples of all
the nations, baptizing them in the name of the*

Awaken to the Moment

*Father and of the Son and of the Holy Spirit,
teaching them to observe all things that I have
commanded you; and lo, I am with you always,
even to the end of the age. Amen."*

Matthew 28:18-20

The power of God's presence can quickly and
easily reverse the damage done by the evil one.
What we need in this hour is a glory encounter
with the living God. We need His living water,
His light, and His power.

If He came that we may have life and have it
more abundantly, then that's what we should
have. He sent His light, His power, His presence, and His glory into the world for change,
and He has called us as agents of that change.

This was His pattern of ministry from the
beginning:

*And when He had called His twelve disciples to
Him, He gave them power over unclean spirits,
to cast them out, and to heal all kinds of sickness
and all kinds of disease.* Matthew 10:1

*And as you go, preach, saying, "The kingdom
of heaven is at hand." Heal the sick, cleanse the*

lepers, raise the dead, cast out demons. Freely you have received, freely give.

Matthew 10:7-8

But I will come to you soon, if the Lord wills, and I shall find out, not the words of those who are arrogant but their power. For the kingdom of God does not consist in words but in power.

1 Corinthians 4:19-20, NASB

God's Kingdom does not consist of mere words. It is a Kingdom of power. When in the wilderness of Judah, David sang:

So I have looked for You in the sanctuary,
To see Your power and Your glory.

Psalm 63:2

That whole passage declares:

O God, You are my God;
Early will I seek You;
My soul thirsts for You;
My flesh longs for You
In a dry and thirsty land
Where there is no water.

Awaken to the Moment

So I have looked for You in the sanctuary,
To see Your power and Your glory.
Because Your lovingkindness is better than life,
My lips shall praise You.
Thus I will bless You while I live;
I will lift up my hands in Your presence!

Psalm 63:1-4

What is this power that David so passionately sought? It is the power to overcome, the power to win, and winning is our destiny:

And they overcame him by the blood of the
Lamb, and by the word of their testimony; and
they loved not their lives unto the death.

Revelation 12:11, KJV

God's authority in our lives gives us the power of oneness, the power of unity, the power of the cross:

But we preach Christ crucified, unto the Jews
a stumblingblock, and unto the Greeks foolish-
ness; but unto them which are called, both Jews
and Greeks, Christ the power of God, and the
wisdom of God. Because the foolishness of God

is wiser than men; and the weakness of God is stronger than men. For ye see your calling, brethren, how that not many wise men after the flesh, not many mighty, not many noble, are called: but God hath chosen the foolish things of the world to confound the wise; and God hath chosen the weak things of the world to confound the things which are mighty; and base things of the world, and things which are despised, hath God chosen, yea, and things which are not, to bring to nought things that are: that no flesh should glory in His presence.

1 Corinthians 1:23-29, KJV

Yes, there is power in unity, power in the cross, power in the very name of Jesus, power in His blood, power in His resurrection, power in His Spirit, power in His Word, power in His presence. And we need His power.

This is the power to win, but it is also the power to change, the power to overcome, the power to heal, the power to save, the power to deliver, the power to gain wealth. We all need this power.

Personally, I want the power and presence of God, and I'm not willing to settle for one without the other. He is looking for men and woman of faith who will contend with Him for the fulfillment of His promises and His Word. He is not afraid or intimidated by our faith to believe for the supernatural or the gifts of the Spirit. He is moved by our faith; our faith pleases God.

Eagle Worldwide Ministries, of which Mave and I are founders, was birthed and built by the power and presence of God. People come to our camp, churches, and special meetings to experience an encounter with Him. This means we can never settle for less, or we will become just another church or religious group. Your church was never meant to be a social club, or a mere religious gathering. It is the House of God.

The Word of God clearly links and syncs the gifts of the Holy Spirit and signs, wonders, and miracles, and the supernatural power of God, the power of the Gospel, to our salvation:

> *How shall we escape if we ignore so great a salvation? This salvation, which was first announced by the Lord, was confirmed to us by those who heard him. God also testified to it by signs, wonders and various miracles, and by*

*gifts of the Holy Spirit distributed according
to his will.*   Hebrews 2:3-4, NIV

Our mission is not about good teaching, good preaching, good music, or good meetings; it's about experiencing and encountering the power and presence of the living God and making sons and daughters for Him. Let us never forget this or settle for less. Let us contend with God for the greater works Jesus spoke of in John 14 and the greater glory that we know is to come.

When I got saved, I didn't understand the Word, but I understood power. And, I knew that I needed the power of the Holy Ghost to help me overcome the life-altering issues and addictions I was facing.

John the Baptist was empowered to bring change in his time:

> *In those days John the Baptist came preaching
> in the wilderness of Judea, and saying, "Repent,
> for the kingdom of heaven is at hand!" For this
> is he who was spoken of by the prophet Isaiah,
> saying:*
> *"The voice of one crying in the wilderness:
> 'Prepare the way of the Lord;*

Make His paths straight.' "
Now John himself was clothed in camel's hair,
with a leather belt around his waist; and his food
was locusts and wild honey. Then Jerusalem,
all Judea, and all the region around the Jordan
went out to him and were baptized by him in
the Jordan, confessing their sins.

Matthew 3:1-6

Real prophets preach repentance and stand for righteousness. Real prophets build altars. They raise up other prophets and prophetic voices; they make sons and daughters. And, of course, they prophesy with accuracy, with power, and with authority.

How can you know a prophet? You will know one when you meet one by their fruit, the fruit of the Spirit, the fruit of their ministry, and the fruit of true discipleship.

In this season, prophets will still take an axe to the root of the trees and will be involved with end-time ministry such as spiritual warfare, deliverance, inner healing, and intercession:

And now also the axe is laid unto the root of
the trees: therefore every tree which bringeth

not forth good fruit is hewn down, and cast into the fire. I indeed baptize you with water unto repentance: but he that cometh after me is mightier than I, whose shoes I am not worthy to bear: he shall baptize you with the Holy Ghost, and with fire: whose fan is in his hand, and he will thoroughly purge his floor, and gather his wheat into the garner; but he will burn up the chaff with unquenchable fire.

Matthew 3:10-12, KJV

Sometimes we prejudge others we know and how they may react to the power of God, the gifts of the Spirit, tabernacle worship, and other manifestations of the power and presence of God. I was a businessman and a Catholic, and yet this is precisely what ministered to me, not the rules, regulations, and rituals of religion.

I was saved in my living room in a season of desperation by God's presence and His love. He baptized me in the Spirit while I was crying out to Him on the side of the road for His power to overcome my life-altering habits and sin. He then taught me by dreams and visions, by a woman in the choir at Brownsville whose head shook for three straight hours, by the incredibly powerful altar calls given there, by the signs, wonders, and miracles I saw, heard about, and experienced at Calvary Pentecostal Campground under the anointed ministry of Ruth Ward Heflin and her revelation of the glory of God. It wasn't mere words that changed my life. It was the power of God.

David sang:

> *Make a joyful shout to the LORD, all you lands!*
> *Serve the LORD with gladness;*
> *Come before His presence with singing.*
> *Know that the LORD, He is God;*
> *It is He who has made us, and not we ourselves;*
> *We are His people and the sheep of His pasture.*
> *Enter into His gates with thanksgiving,*
> *And into His courts with praise.*
> *Be thankful to Him, and bless His name.*
> *For the LORD is good;*
> *His mercy is everlasting,*
> *And His truth endures to all generations.*
>
> Psalm 100:1-5

Ruth Heflin had a now revelation of Habakkuk 2:14 concerning the knowledge of the glory of the Lord, and I'm thankful that I got to know her:

For the earth shall be filled with the knowledge of the glory of Jehovah, as the waters cover the sea. Habakkuk 2:14, ASV

Oh, the glory! There is nothing like it to bring needed change.

Today, the Lord is raising up an end-time army, a royal priesthood, and restoring His spiritual family, the Church. Yes, we are a royal priesthood, a holy nation of glory carriers, torchbearers who will bring an understanding of cultivating and living in His glorious presence and operating in His power and under His authority.

We are to fulfill the Messianic mandate of Isaiah 60:

Arise, shine; for thy light is come, and the glory of Jehovah is risen upon thee. For, behold, darkness shall cover the earth, and gross darkness the peoples; but Jehovah will arise upon thee, and his glory shall be seen upon thee. And nations shall come to thy light, and kings to the brightness of thy rising.

Lift up thine eyes round about, and see: they all gather themselves together, they come to thee;

*thy sons shall come from far, and thy daughters
shall be carried in the arms. Then thou shalt see
and be radiant, and thy heart shall thrill and be
enlarged; because the abundance of the sea shall
be turned unto thee, the wealth of the nations
shall come unto thee. The multitude of camels
shall cover thee, the dromedaries of Midian and
Ephah; all they from Sheba shall come; they
shall bring gold and frankincense, and shall
proclaim the praises of Jehovah.*

Isaiah 60:1-6, ASV

How will it be accomplished? Through the
preaching the Gospel of the Kingdom in word
and, perhaps more importantly, in the demonstration of God's power and authority.

In recent years, we have experienced the
amazing manifestations of God's glory. His
glory is His presence, and it reveals to us His
power.

One of the biblical words translated *glory* is
shekinah. The word *shekinah* is a transliteration of
a Hebrew word meaning "the one who dwells"
or "that which dwells" and was used to describe
the light on the Mercy Seat in the Ark of the
Covenant that was kept in the Holy of Holies.

My whole heart in this season is to establish a dwelling place for God, for His presence, and for His power.

All prophets are called to build altars wherever they go. First, I want to build an altar in my heart to the Lord. My wife, Mave, wrote in one of her books about living with a prophet and about my unusual times of prayer, intimacy with God, and warfare against the enemy. That is the life I am called to.

The *shekinah* symbolizes the divine presence. The word *shekinah* is not found in scripture, but the root word *shakan* is, and it means "to dwell, to settle down, to tabernacle with, to have a habitation." This word and a related one, *mishkan,* translated into English as *"tabernacle,"* are both frequently used in the Bible, and both are associated with the presence of God (and His glory) dwelling with man.

The meaning of the word *shekinah* (the One Who dwells) reminds us that we did not seek to dwell with God, but He with us, and this truth should evoke continual thanksgiving in those who have been brought into covenant with Him under the shelter of His wings.

In Exodus, we see that it was God who first

expressed His desire to dwell among men. He instructed Moses to tell the people to construct a sanctuary for Him, so that He could dwell *[shakan]* among them:

> *Then have them make a sanctuary for me, and*
> *I will dwell among them.*   Exodus 25:8

Another Bible word for glory is *chayil* (pronounced ca heel). It is "a force, whether of men, means or other resources; an army, wealth, virtue, valor, strength: able, activity, (+) army, band of men (soldiers), company, (great) forces, goods, host, might, power, riches, strength, strong, substance, train, (+)valiant(-ly), valour, virtuous(-ly), war, worthy(-ily)."[1]

Strong's Hebrew Lexicon says of *chayil* that it is "strength, might, efficiency, wealth, army ability, force, might ... valiant."[2] One example might be the power God gave Gideon to make him a *"mighty man of valor."* Gideon looked at himself as weak and a failure. He told God he came from the weakest tribe, and he was weak among that tribe. God's answer was that Gideon should go in the strength He had given him.

1. *Strong's Exhaustive Concordance:* H2428
2. Peabody, MA, Hendrickson Publishing: 2009

"Am I not with you?" God challenged. In our weakness, God will show Himself strong, and you and He together can do all things. If you are willing and obedient and go, you will eat of the fruit of the land, the fruit of the promise.

Reflect on Gideon's experience:

> *And there came an angel of the* LORD, *and sat under an oak which was in Ophrah, that pertained unto Joash the Abiezrite: and his son Gideon threshed wheat by the winepress, to hide it from the Midianites. And the angel of the* LORD *appeared unto him, and said unto him, The* LORD *is with thee, thou mighty man of valour.*
>
> *And Gideon said unto him, Oh my Lord, if the* LORD *be with us, why then is all this befallen us? and where be all his miracles which our fathers told us of, saying, Did not the* LORD *bring us up from Egypt? but now the* LORD *hath forsaken us, and delivered us into the hands of the Midianites.*
>
> *And the* LORD *looked upon him, and said, Go in this thy might, and thou shalt save Israel from the hand of the Midianites: have not I sent thee? And he said unto him, Oh my Lord, wherewith*

shall I save Israel? behold, my family is poor in Manasseh, and I am the least in my father's house. And the LORD said unto him, Surely I will be with thee, and thou shalt smite the Midianites as one man.

And he said unto him, If now I have found grace in thy sight, then shew me a sign that thou talkest with me. Judges 6:11-17, KJV

One of the finest verses in the Scriptures concerning the power of God is found in the book of Acts, and that is New Testament territory.

But ye shall receive power, after that the Holy Ghost is come upon you: and ye shall be witnesses unto me both in Jerusalem, and in all Judaea, and in Samaria, and unto the uttermost part of the earth. Acts 1:8, KJV

That is the power of God's glory. *Chayil* glory is the manifested power and glory of the Lord Jesus Christ in and through His servants. It is power to witness. In context, that verse reads:

For John truly baptized with water; but ye shall be baptized with the Holy Ghost not many days hence.

When they therefore were come together, they asked of him, saying, Lord, wilt thou at this time restore again the kingdom to Israel?

And he said unto them, It is not for you to know the times or the seasons, which the Father hath put in his own power. But ye shall receive power, after that the Holy Ghost is come upon you: and ye shall be witnesses unto me both in Jerusalem, and in all Judaea, and in Samaria, and unto the uttermost part of the earth.

Acts 1:5-8, KJV

In Acts 2, it is recorded that when the Spirit fell upon those early believers, they went right out and started witnessing. That was the promise:

And it shall come to pass in the last days, saith God, I will pour out of my Spirit upon all flesh: and your sons and your daughters shall prophesy, and your young men shall see visions, and your old men shall dream dreams: and on my servants and on my handmaidens I will pour out in those days of my Spirit; and they shall prophesy: and I will shew wonders in heaven above, and signs in the earth beneath; blood, and fire, and vapour of smoke: the sun shall be turned into darkness, and the moon into blood, before that great and notable day of the Lord come: and it shall come to pass, that whosoever shall call on the name of the Lord shall be saved. Ye men of Israel, hear these words; Jesus of Nazareth, a man approved of God among you by miracles and wonders and signs, which God did by him in the midst of you, as ye yourselves also know. Acts 2:17-22, KJV

This is the power to save, heal, deliver, and overcome the enemy.

God is practical and wants to empower us, giving us the power to win, the power to overcome, the power of His Holy Spirit. The early believers prayed for this power and fully expected signs, wonders, and miracles:

Now, Lord, consider their threats and enable your servants to speak your word with great boldness. Stretch out your hand to heal and perform signs and wonders through the name of your holy servant Jesus.

Acts 4:29-30, NIV

When Jesus came to Earth, the Spirit of the Lord was upon Him to fulfill the words of Isaiah 11:1-2:

> *And there shall come forth a rod out of the stem of Jesse, and a Branch shall grow out of his roots: and the spirit of the LORD shall rest upon him, the spirit of wisdom and understanding, the spirit of counsel and might, the spirit of knowledge and of the fear of the LORD.*
>
> Isaiah 11:1-2, KJV

Jesus had the Spirit of might, wisdom, counsel, and a sound mind. Then, at Pentecost, those who had believed on Him received the gifts of the Spirit—prophecy, dreams, and visions. We need times of refreshing in God's presence, and this is the season we're in, the restoration of all things, the biblical model of the emerging twenty-first century end-time church.

What did the Lord say about *"times of refreshing"*? He said that revival would come from the presence of the Lord until the restoration of all things, and then the Lord would return.

Paul accurately foretold of this end-times season. He said that religious people would deny the power of God, not necessarily the existence of His presence, but *"the power thereof"*:

> *This know also, that in the last days perilous times shall come. For men shall be lovers of their own selves, covetous, boasters, proud, blasphemers, disobedient to parents, unthankful, unholy, Without natural affection, trucebreakers, false accusers, incontinent, fierce, despisers of those that are good, traitors, heady, highminded, lovers of pleasures the more than lovers of God; having a form of godliness, but denying the power thereof: from such turn away. For of this sort are they which creep into houses, and lead captive silly women laden with sins, led away with divers lusts, ever learning, and never able to come to the knowledge of the truth.*
>
> 2 Timothy 3:1-7, KJV

Let us go forth to preach the Gospel of the Kingdom, which includes righteousness, holiness, hope, consecration, sanctification, Heaven, and Hell. If you leave any of this out, yours is a watered-downed gospel with no true power. Today, you might as well throw out the Ten Commandments. Which one of them do you think God no longer considers a sin? Or let's throw out all offensive Old and New Testament scriptures, scriptures like these:

Or do you not know that the unrighteous will not inherit the kingdom of God? Do not be deceived: neither the sexually immoral, nor idolaters, nor adulterers, nor men who practice homosexuality, nor thieves, nor the greedy, nor drunkards, nor revilers, nor swindlers will inherit the kingdom of God.
1 Corinthians 6:9-10, ESV

You shall not lie with a male as with a woman; it is an abomination.   Leviticus 18:22, ESV

For this reason God gave them up to dishonorable passions. For their women exchanged natural relations for those that are contrary to nature; and the men likewise gave up natural relations with women and were consumed with passion for one another, men committing shameless acts with men and receiving in themselves the due penalty for their error.
Romans 1:26-27, ESV

Awaken to the Moment

If a man lies with a male as with a woman, both of them have committed an abomination; they shall surely be put to death; their blood is upon them.   Leviticus 20:13, ESV

No, it's all valid and useful. We must *Awaken to the Moment*, going forth to preach the full Gospel of the Kingdom of God, for there is power and authority in that Word. This is a *Kingdom Reality*.

Thank You, Lord, for giving us all the power and authority we need to overcome and that the power in us is greater than the power in the world. I ask You to teach our hands to war and give us revelation wisdom and understanding of how to apply it in our daily lives. I release the anointing of end-time warriors and handmaidens over us right now and declare a fresh revelation of who we are, more than conquerors in Christ Jesus. I declare the now moment for the Army of God to arise and shine, that the day of breakthrough and victory is at hand, that the powerful right hand of the Lord is on the shoulder of the remnant in this moment, releasing His favor, that He has dispatched angels to assist us and to fulfill the destiny of God in our lives, and that we are the generation marked for victory and to prepare the way and usher in the Second Coming of Christ.

Amen!

TODAY

THE LORD

IS RAISING UP

AN END-TIME ARMY,

A ROYAL PRIESTHOOD,

AND RESTORING

HIS SPIRITUAL FAMILY,

THE CHURCH!

Chapter 8

Running to Win the Prize

*Do you not know that those who run in a race
all run, but one receives the prize? Run in such
a way that you may obtain it. And everyone who
competes for the prize is temperate in all things.
Now they do it to obtain a perishable crown, but
we for an imperishable crown. Therefore I run
thus: not with uncertainty. Thus I fight: not
as one who beats the air. But I discipline my
body and bring it into subjection, lest, when I
have preached to others, I myself should become
disqualified.* 1 Corinthians 9:24-27

Let us awaken with purpose, as men and women,
sons and daughters, and run the race, striving for
the crown. We know that we cannot buy or win or
compete for the greatest prize, the greatest miracle

of all. It is a gift. Our salvation was purchased for us and given to us as a free gift that we receive by grace through faith in the Lord Jesus Christ. Why? So that no man can ever say he earned his way to Heaven or to eternal life.

> *For by grace you have been saved through faith, and that not of yourselves; it is the gift of God, not of works, lest anyone should boast. For we are His workmanship, created in Christ Jesus for good works, which God prepared beforehand that we should walk in them.*   Ephesians 2:8-10

Yes, we are only saved by grace through faith in the Lord.

Let us also understand the purpose of our salvation was not Heaven alone, but to do good works here in the Earth, to bring Heaven's blessings to Earth. So we are saved by grace for the purpose of good works:

> *Thus says the Lord:*

> *"Let not the wise man glory in his wisdom,*
> *Let not the mighty man glory in his might,*
> *Nor let the rich man glory in his riches;"*
>   Jeremiah 9:23

What should we boast in?

"But let him who glories glory in this,
That he understands and knows Me,
That I am the Lord, *exercising lovingkindness,*
judgment, and righteousness in the earth.
For in these I delight," says the Lord.

Jeremiah 9:24

In my opinion, this is the high calling of God!
Consider this too: When the seventy that Jesus
sent out returned with great victory, Jesus said
to them, *"Rejoice because your names are written in*
heaven":

Then the seventy returned with joy, saying,
"Lord, even the demons are subject to us in
Your name."
And He said to them, "I saw Satan fall like
lightning from heaven. Behold, I give you the
authority to trample on serpents and scorpions,
and over all the power of the enemy, and noth-
ing shall by any means hurt you. Nevertheless
do not rejoice in this, that the spirits are subject
to you, but rather rejoice because your names
are written in heaven.   Luke 10:17-20

Awaken to the Moment

Paul spoke very directly and very clearly under the power of the Holy Spirit about running the race with purpose to obtain the prize, but his efforts were not like the world or for worldly reward—the earthly, carnal, and temporal, but for things that are incorruptible and everlasting. It is time that you and I ran to win this race. The writer of Hebrews tells us:

> *Therefore, since we are surrounded by so great a cloud of witnesses, let us also lay aside every weight, and sin which clings so closely, and let us run with endurance the race that is set before us.* Hebrews 12:1, ESV

What awaits the faithful? Crowns. David, the great psalmist, the great warrior, the great worshipper, the greatest King Israel ever had, said it this way:

> *For the Lord takes delight in his people;*
> *he crowns the humble with victory.*
> *Let his faithful people rejoice in this honor*
> *and sing for joy on their beds.*
> Psalm 149:4-5, NIV

There are other crowns mentioned in the Scriptures:

- The Crown of Victory that goes to the humble and faithful
- The Crown of Life
- An incorruptible, imperishable crown
- The Crown of Righteousness
- The Crown of Glory
- The Crown of Rejoicing

All of us run the race, but do we run to win? Win what? With what? And what wins? Let's take a closer look.

The Crown of Righteousness:

I have fought the good fight, I have finished the race, I have kept the faith. Finally, there is laid up for me the crown of righteousness, which the Lord, the righteous Judge, will give to me on that Day, and not to me only but also to all who have loved His appearing. 2 Timothy 4:7-8

The Crown of Life:

Blessed is the man who endures temptation; for when he has been approved, he will receive the crown of life which the Lord has promised to those who love Him. James 1:12

The Crown of Glory:

The elders who are among you I exhort, I who am a fellow elder and a witness of the sufferings of Christ, and also a partaker of the glory that will be revealed: Shepherd the flock of God which is among you, serving as overseers, not by compulsion but willingly, not for dishonest gain but eagerly; nor as being lords over those entrusted to you, but being examples to the flock; and when the Chief Shepherd appears, you will receive the crown of glory that does not fade away. 1 Peter 5:1-4

The Incorruptible Crown, also known as the Imperishable Crown:

And everyone who competes for the prize is temperate in all things. Now they do it to obtain a perishable crown, but we for an imperishable crown. 1 Corinthians 9:25

Paul deemed this crown *"imperishable"* in order to contrast it with the temporal awards his contemporaries pursued.

Finally, the Crown of Rejoicing:

For what is our hope, or joy, or crown of rejoicing? Is it not even you in the presence of our Lord Jesus Christ at His coming?
1 Thessalonians 2:19

This is a soul-winners crown, and is available to all believers who strive to win souls:

Therefore, my beloved and longed-for brethren, my joy and crown, so stand fast in the Lord, beloved. Philippians 4:1

This crown is given to those who engage in the evangelization of those outside the Church. Paul earned this crown after winning the Thessalonians to faith in Jesus. Let us strive, pressing ever toward the goal to win this crown.

Awaken to the Moment

Our greatest prize is to know Jesus and yearn for citizenship in Heaven. Paul yearned for this greatest of prizes:

> *That I may know Him and the power of His resurrection, and the fellowship of His sufferings, being conformed to His death, if, by any means, I may attain to the resurrection from the dead. Not that I have already attained, or am already perfected; but I press on, that I may lay hold of that for which Christ Jesus has also laid hold of me.*
>
> *Brethren, I do not count myself to have apprehended; but one thing I do, forgetting those things which are behind and reaching forward to those things which are ahead, I press toward the goal for the prize of the upward call of God in Christ Jesus.*
>
> *Therefore let us, as many as are mature, have this mind; and if in anything you think otherwise, God will reveal even this to you. Nevertheless, to the degree that we have already attained, let us walk by the same rule, let us be of the same mind.*
>
> *Brethren, join in following my example, and note those who so walk, as you have us for a*

pattern. For many walk, of whom I have told you often, and now tell you even weeping, that they are the enemies of the cross of Christ: whose end is destruction, whose god is their belly, and whose glory is in their shame—who set their mind on earthly things. For our citizenship is in heaven, from which we also eagerly wait for the Savior, the Lord Jesus Christ, who will transform our lowly body that it may be conformed to His glorious body, according to the working by which He is able even to subdue all things to Himself.   Philippians 3:10-21

Beloved, we must *Awaken to the Moment*, for the race is serious, and we must obtain the prize. This is a *Kingdom Reality*.

PRAYER:

Here we are, Lord, the called, the chosen, and the faithful, in all of our weaknesses and shortcomings, running our race of faith, doing everything we can and trusting that You will do everything we cannot. Help us to work and walk in unity and harmony with the generations. Help us to touch our roots and reach our destiny. In the eyes of this world, we are foolishness. Strengthen us, equip us, prepare us, and train us to rule and reign with love and humility and to finish well!

In Jesus' name.

THE PURPOSE OF OUR SALVATION WAS NOT HEAVEN ALONE, BUT TO DO GOOD WORKS HERE ON THE EARTH, TO BRING HEAVEN'S BLESSINGS TO EARTH! SO, WE ARE SAVED BY GRACE FOR THE PURPOSE OF GOOD WORKS!

Chapter 9

The Maturing of Marketplace Ministries

Why did you seek Me? Did you not know that
I must be about My Father's business?

Luke 2:49

Mave and I both spent more than twenty years in business and marketplace ministry long before it was recognized as a viable part of church and missionary work. Mave worked in the restaurant business and in entertainment, and I was in sports, the security business, and television before hearing the Lord calling us into full-time pulpit ministry. We both used our businesses to be evangelistic and to impact our communities through outreach, shows, and practical training programs to promote the Gospel.

Awaken to the Moment

Since being in full-time ministry, we have continued to invest our time and experience, training, mentoring, equipping, and working with marketplace ministers in the last twenty-five years, and we see marketplace ministry coming into a season of maturity and fruitfulness.

Over the years, as Christians working outside the nuclear church environment began a marketplace ministry, they often lacked strategy, planning, and structure; they also lacked fruit. Other Christians thought their bounty from business was only for them and their family, and so they had little or no real Kingdom impact.

The Seven Mountains strategy for the harvest had a great impact in forming vision and explaining purpose. However, too many Christians were not readily engaged as ministers, nor were they equipped by the church and practically trained to reign in the marketplace, to witness and let their light shine and to be God's face in the marketplace. I am very happy to report that things are improving dramatically. Many have now embraced the call, developed relations and ministry momentum, and are now beginning to take ground in the Kingdom. I've even seen many of them employ intercessors and build workplace teams of real disciples and, thus, have a lasting impact.

In some cases, they have birthed Bible studies and formed prayer and care groups. They are also forming stronger ties between the church and marketplace. The result is that many churches are thriving and having a real and essential impact on their community and those in need.

Yes, marketplace ministry is coming of age just in time for the harvest that I feel will be reaped through the Church. This will bring an awakening to our society, as men and women recognize us by our love and caring of others and one another. Love always wins the day! As we step into this incredible moment, we must be about the Father's business.

When Jesus was just twelve, He made a great pilgrimage to Jerusalem with His parents, relatives, and friends. When the festivities had ended and the company was returning home, He was found missing. When located, He said to Mary and Joseph: *"Why did you seek Me? Did you not know that I must be about My Father's business?"*

(Luke 2:49). Verse 50 records the reaction of those He addressed:

> *But they did not understand the statement which He spoke to them.* Luke 2:50

For some reason, today we still have trouble understanding when men and women are called of God and want to step out into the Father's business. Regardless of whether it is within the typical nuclear church setting, the marketplace, or the mission field, when we answer that call to separate ourselves for the work God has called us to, there comes an awkward season of transition in our lives and with our close relationships.

Each of us is called personally and is unique in many ways, and each of us brings who we are to the table of service to God. The talents, giftings, time, energy, and callings are unique and make a place for us. The Lord has a place that He has prepared just for you, a place of protection, a place of provision, a place of celebration, a place where you fit perfectly.

This doesn't mean there will not be obstacles and hindrances to overcome and battles to be fought and won. That is all part of the process of the making and molding of the heart of a disciple and leader, and it all happens in the furnace of adversity. We need to embrace an understanding of the priesthood of the believer.

What did Jesus do when He was misunderstood?

Then He went down with them and came to Nazareth, and was subject to them, but His mother kept all these things in her heart. And Jesus increased in wisdom and stature, and in favor with God and men. Luke 2:51-52

It is very important to our future that we operate in godly and biblical Kingdom principles and that we do so with integrity, character, and faithfulness. As we do, others will see that we are not merely a hearer of the Word but a real doer, sincere, kind, and caring regardless of the challenges we face. We must remain loyal, faithful, and hardworking team players who advance and enhance the company and its values.

I received a prophetic alert in the fall of 2022 and released it on Friday, October 28 of that year:

PROPHETIC ALERT

Radical change is coming to the nation in the next seventy days!

Here's how this alert came about. In Matthew 24, Jesus spoke of *"the beginning of sorrows."* I was taken up in an open vision. In the vision, there was a big warehouse, and in the warehouse was an old-fashioned printing press. It had a big roller drum, and that drum kept rolling and rolling and rolling until it had flattened everything in sight. People, things, objects of this world (idols) were being flattened.

Then I began to see an open window, and printed newspapers were flying out the window. There was a counting mechanism, and it registered 70. Then the Lord said, "During the next 70 days, you will hear announcements that will radically change the nation. This will radically change the way media looks and the way media works. I'm going to go deep inside the thing and flatten everything that's not of Me. Change is coming, and so is transformation. I'm hard at work behind the scenes, and I'm filling the house even now."

Then the Lord took me up in the air, and I saw Nazareth as an old village. There was a donkey walking around and around in a crude sort of press. Then the Lord said to me, "The new wine is being made right now. My people have been crushed, but they have been prepared for this season. Know that the remnant will come out with fresh new wine and a fresh new anointing in this hour."

As I have noted elsewhere, it will get worse before it gets better—a lot worse, but in the end, we win. In the midst of the anarchy, chaos, change, and transition, a transformation is taking place with the twenty-first century Church, the emerging Church, the Remnant. The true *Ekklesia* will rise from the ashes.

We work closely with a few para-church marketplace ministries. These include Full Gospel Business Men's Fellowship International, political groups, and the Band of Brothers that are having a wonderful season of Spirit-filled harvest. We also work with The Centre 4 Excellence, the Kingsway, and Eagle Worldwide Community Enrichment, and their work of feeding the hungry, housing the homeless, and reaching out to those outside the four walls.

Awaken to the Moment

They are being the real Church in action. Please keep these in your prayers. They are ministering at the place where the rubber meets the road. We need to pray for, support, and encourage anyone ministering in the marketplace.

Many people have come to me concerning prophetic economic insight. I sometimes share what I feel is the Lord on a certain matter and, occasionally, when asked, bring advice, but I think it's important that we clearly differentiate between "thus saith the Lord" and my feelings or thoughts on a matter. In order for us to restore the prophetic gift and office gift of the prophet, we need integrity, character, honor, honesty, and protocol both in the marketplace and the church. I also believe that prophetic people should, in no way, sell or charge for such information, as one would as a consultant or advisor. We need to make sure that the man or woman, the Gospel, and the gifts are not for sale.

I have often spoken of gold and silver, along with balance and prayer, when people are making their investment choices in this vulnerable season. Since this current downturn began in 2020, the value of the dollar is down some 25% to 30%, while gold and silver are continuing to rise. Each person's situation and financial goals and needs are quite different, and each should make important decisions after personal prayer and personal revelation from God geared toward their economic objectives and condition.

When I mentioned maturity in the marketplace, I remember in the early season many of the errors and pitfalls experienced and later used to discredit the prophetic in areas such as Ponzi schemes, limited partner real estate deals, and other get-rich-quick pie-in-the-sky concepts. Normally speaking, if it looks too good to be true, it probably is. I, for one, want to use the systematic biblical principles of sowing and giving, along with a strong work ethic. I know that God rewards diligence and faith, and His promises are *yeah* and *amen*.

I know God wants to bless and prosper us as our soul prospers and that He is the one who gives us the power to gain wealth, influence, and wisdom. He blesses us, as He did Abraham, to be a blessing. Also, He is looking in this season for people He can trust to fund the Kingdom and end-time ministries. He can get wealth to you if He knows He can get it through you and into His Kingdom purposes in this hour.

I use four biblical models that Mark Gorman highlighted in his book, *God's Plan for Prosperity*,[1] along with a number of other principles and means. I want to know why, how, and what I can biblically expect. I also want to be balanced, systematic, and not led by emotions, but by the Spirit and the Word.

I continually check my motives, always wanting to sow out of a heart of love and appreciation, never out of fear, compulsion, manipulation, or selfish gain, but a heart for God, His children, and His Kingdom. The Lord has been so wonderful, always showering us with His blessings. Here are four secrets to prosperity:

1) **Giving Alms:** God's promise is that you will not go without in your time of need when you purpose in your heart to give with compassion for those in need. I give into good Kingdom causes and lives, such as to feed the hungry, house the homeless, the underprivileged, widows, orphans, human trafficking victims, etc. God provides to me to give into the needs of others.

---

1. (New Orleans, LA, Mark Gorman.com: 2004)

2) **Paying the Tithe:** This breaks the curse off of our finances and opens the windows of Heaven. The tithe (10% of your income) belongs to God, not to me. I sow it into the church or ministry where I am called to serve and receive.

3) **Giving First Fruits:** God's promise is that He will fill our vats with new wine. I use this when starting new ventures or in new seasons or sowing into ministries that are pioneering, particularly at times when I am pressing and believing for a similar or parallel vision.

4) **Practicing Seedtime and Harvest:** This is when I am believing for a supernatural return, and I am looking to sow into some Kingdom focus that is very fertile, faith-based, and like-hearted.

Here are a few principles I try to adhere to in every situation. I want to sow joyfully, sow in faith, and sow in obedience. I want to be lavish in my giving and with an expectation of the promise related and connected to the principle or the moment. I always want to be open-minded and open-hearted to hear the prompting of the Spirit of God. I also sow into my harvest field or a field on my heart that I may want to have an impact in. Many times, when I sow my seed, I will write on the envelope specific needs that I have, and I name my seeds at times like a farmer, always expecting my harvest. Then I tend my garden by watering it with prayer and declaration.

I know that God is faithful to those who diligently seek Him. I know that He is moved by our faith, obedience, and faithfulness. I know that it is His good pleasure to bless us, and I know that I cannot outgive Him. It's His nature and pleasure to bless us. I also know that He is the One who give me the power to gain wealth and that He wants me to prosper as my soul prospers. So, I want to continue to nurture myself in my relationship with God and assure my personal spiritual growth and development. I look forward to offering time as an opportunity to open up a fresh flow of blessing in my life.

Finally, I know that my seed is not just money. My time, effort, energy, talent, ability, creativity, encouraging words, and good deeds can all be considered seed. I am sure that I can never outgive God and that He is the Lord of the harvest and His heart is on my seed.

For sure, I can never outgive God. If I come with a spoon, He will come with a shovel. If I come with a shovel, He will come with a front-end loader. I only have to concern myself with my faithfulness, because His name and nature is Faithful and True. I love it when I feel God is asking for something of importance or value in my life as a sacrifice. I joyfully give it and then stand in faith, hope, and expectation on the promise of Mark 10:

Then Jesus looked around and said to His disciples, "How hard it is for those who have riches to enter the kingdom of God!" And the disciples were astonished at His words. But Jesus answered again and said to them, "Children, how hard it is for those who trust in riches to enter the kingdom of God! It is easier for a camel to go through the eye of a needle than for a rich man to enter the kingdom of God."

And they were greatly astonished, saying among themselves, "Who then can be saved?" But Jesus looked at them and said, "With men it is impossible, but not with God; for with God all things are possible."

Then Peter began to say to Him, "See, we have left all and followed You."

So Jesus answered and said, "Assuredly, I say to you, there is no one who has left house or brothers or sisters or father or mother or wife or children or lands, for My sake and the gospel's, who shall not receive a hundredfold now in this time—houses and brothers and sisters and mothers and children and lands, with persecutions—and in the age to come, eternal life. But many who are first will be last, and the last first."   Mark 10:23-31

Yes, we must *Awaken to the Moment*, for the harvest is great and must be reaped out where the souls are. This is a *Kingdom Reality*.

PRAYER:

Father, I pray now for all of those called into ministry in the marketplace, those called to be Your voice, Your hands, Your feet, those called to reflect Your face in the marketplace. I ask that You bless them today as they step into the place You've established for them. Let their gift make a place for them. I ask that You confirm their calling and refresh and revive the vision and mission You've given them. Let Your blessings and favor rest upon them, and light a fresh fire in their hearts. Thank You!

In Jesus' name,
Amen!

THIS

IS

FOR

SURE:

I

CAN

NEVER

OUTGIVE

GOD!

Chapter 10

Settling Issues of Identity

And Jesus came and spoke to them, saying, "All authority has been given to Me in heaven and on earth. Go therefore and make disciples of all the nations, baptizing them in the name of the Father and of the Son and of the Holy Spirit, teaching them to observe all things that I have commanded you; and lo, I am with you always, even to the end of the age. Amen."

Matthew 28:18-20

Have you ever wondered why our world is so mixed up? What's going on? Is it me? The culture? The media? The educational system? The government? The church? Well, probably all of the above plus some other influences. However, it all starts and finishes with you and me and the other members of the Body of Christ. We have the power, authority, and responsibility to change things. We are the true change-makers, the history makers of our generation. According to the Great Commission given us by Jesus in Matthew 28:18-20, we have been given all power and all authority.

This was the same way Jesus sent out the twelve and also the seventy-two:

> *Then He called His twelve disciples together and gave them power and authority over all demons, and to cure diseases. He sent them to preach the kingdom of God and to heal the sick.* Luke 9:1-2

> *After this the Lord appointed seventy-two[a] others and sent them two by two ahead of him to every town and place where he was about to go. He told them, "The harvest is plentiful, but the workers are few. Ask the Lord of the harvest, therefore, to send out workers into his harvest field. Go! I am sending you out like lambs among wolves.* Luke 10:1-3

Let's you and I take a little walk together with the Holy Spirit to get a closer look at this major issue facing us, our families, our nations and society today. Who are we?

The Kingdom reality is that we are a new creation in Christ Jesus. North America and the world are having identity issues because we, the Body of Christ, either do not understand or are not yet living in the reality of our true identity in Christ. According to the Word of God, we have another Helper, the Comforter, the Spirit of Truth, that the world doesn't know, doesn't see, or doesn't receive. He is with us to lead us, guide us, direct us, protect us, and teach us all things:

> *He will give you another Helper, that He may abide with you forever—the Spirit of truth, whom the world cannot receive, because it neither sees Him nor knows Him.*
>
> John 14:16-17

When asked about our societal issues, Pastor Tony Evans said earlier this year, "Our identity is rooted in the spirit and the image of God, but we've gotten so ingrained in the thinking of the culture that we wind up being parakeets to what the society is saying, rather than taking a solid, loving, but clear stance on what God is saying."[1] There is power in the Word and in the Spirit, and they agree. We can overcome this and any other obstacle and hindrance that opposes us. We are overcomers and more than conquers in Christ.

Our identity is settled! We are sons and daughters of God, not slaves and servants, but sons and daughters with a servant's heart. There is no mention of any other human creation in the Scriptures. We are either a son or a daughter. We are also made kings and priests unto God through Christ Jesus:

> *And from Jesus Christ, who is the faithful witness, and the first begotten of the dead, and the prince of the kings of the earth. Unto him that loved us, and washed us from our sins in his own blood, and hath made us kings and priests unto God and his Father; to him be glory and dominion for ever and ever. Amen.*
>
> Revelation 1:5-6, KJV

John the Revelator declared, in Revelation 5, the new song, the new you, the new creation

---

1. From a radio program I heard.

reality, and the fact that we are indeed kings and priests:

> *And they sung a new song, saying, Thou art worthy to take the book, and to open the seals thereof: for thou wast slain, and hast redeemed us to God by thy blood out of every kindred, and tongue, and people, and nation; and hast made us unto our God kings and priests: and we shall reign on the earth.*　Revelation 5:9-10, KJV

We are joint heirs with Christ, never to be in bondage or fear. The Spirit of God declares our identity and our inheritance in Christ:

> *For as many as are led by the Spirit of God, they are the sons of God. For ye have not received the spirit of bondage again to fear; but ye have received the Spirit of adoption, whereby we cry, Abba, Father. The Spirit itself beareth witness with our spirit, that we are the children of God: and if children, then heirs; heirs of God, and joint-heirs with Christ; if so be that we suffer with him, that we may be also glorified together.*　Romans 8:14-17, KJV

Awaken to the Moment

All of creation is awaiting our arrival and rising to the occasion, knowing who we are and anticipating our revealing as sons led by the Spirit in this moment.

> *For the earnest expectation of the creation eagerly waits for the revealing of the sons of God.*
> Romans 8:19

> *For as many as are led by the Spirit of God, these are sons of God.* Romans 8:14

If you are in a battle and being challenged by an enemy or the reality of the moment or your own weakness and shortcomings, read all of Romans chapter 8 over and over. There you will find many strong biblical confirmations of who Christ made us and how He views us. From a practical application standpoint, turn these promises into declarations and declare them over yourself regularly morning and night. Do it particularly at the point of the battle, conflict, or uncertainty. Then praise God for your identity and who He says you are any and every time the avenger attacks you with his lies. Fight as David instructed us to fight:

LORD, our LORD,
  how majestic is your name in all the earth!
You have set your glory
  in the heavens.
Through the praise of children and infants
    you have established a stronghold against
your enemies,
    to silence the foe and the avenger.
                                   Psalm 8:1-2, NIV

I use a daily covering prayer that includes declarations, as well as taking authority over curses and spirits that are opposing our true identity. The finished work of Christ on the cross, the blood He shed, the price He paid, and the promises He made are clear and enough to ensure our true identity. However, we must fight and contend with the spiritual weapons He has given us when the enemy comes to lie to us, and kill and destroy our hopes, our vision, our destiny, and our identity.

We cannot listen to or agree with the enemy, the world, or our own feelings. Rather, we must come into agreement and alignment with God and His Word. We must guard our hearts by being careful of what we see, hear, and receive, as

177

well as the people we associate with and listen to. Why? Because faith comes by hearing:

> *So then faith comes by hearing, and hearing by the word of God.* Romans 10:17

Yes, faith comes by hearing, and so does doubt. Words are a powerful force, either positive or negative. We must use wisdom and discernment. Choose life or death. Choose good friends, partners, and relationships, as well as have healthy boundaries to guard your heart, so that you can live out this Kingdom reality and your true identity.

Let us purpose here and now to dig deep in relationship with God, in the name and promises of the Son, and allow the Holy Spirit to pull out our divine destiny and God-given talents, giftings, and abilities.

This may sound as simple as believing, but I honestly believe that if we are to succeed in our quest for true freedom and identity, we need to step into our place in the Body of Christ and be properly discipled and aligned.

Many times we may need freedom ministry, deliverance, inner healing, good pastoral care or counselling along the way. Therefore, we must be fully engaged in the family of God so that we can build a structure in our Christian walk and then bear the fruit of our salvation and sonship. This involves receiving the paternity of the Father through establishing a solid prayer life, along with developing a deep personal relationship with Christ. We must study and practice the Word of God with diligence and receive the true healing and acceptance that can only be found in His heart.

The enemy wants to make sure you don't ever really get to know who you are. I declare sonship and daughterhood over you right now. I declare that you are no longer a stranger but a citizen in the household God, made in the righteousness of God, declared righteous through Christ, and are a new creation in Him. May you fulfill your destiny in Christ and leave a legacy that lives on long after you are gone.

We must *Awaken to the Moment*, for the signs of the times are all around us. This is a *Kingdom Reality*.

PRAYER:

I am God's child, I resist the devil, and no weapon formed against me shall prosper. I put on the whole armor of God and take authority over this day in Jesus' name. Let it be prosperous for me and let me walk in Your love. The Holy Spirit leads and guides me, and I am able to discern between the righteous and the wicked. I take authority over Satan, all his demons, and all people influenced by them, and I declare that Satan is under my feet and shall remain there all day.

I am the righteousness of God in Christ Jesus. I am God's property. Satan, you are bound from my family, my mind, my body, my home, and my finances. I confess that I am healed and whole. I flourish, am long-lived, stable, durable, incorruptible, fruitful, virtuous, and full of peace, patience, and love. Whatsoever I set my hands to do shall prosper, for God supplies all my needs. I have all authority over Satan, all demons and beasts of the field.

God, I pray for the ministry You have for me. Anoint me for all You have called me to do for You. I call forth divine appointments, open doors of opportunity, God-ordained encounters and ministry positions. I claim a hedge of protection around myself, and my spouse and children throughout this day and night. I ask You, God, in the name of Jesus, to dispatch angels to surround me, my spouse, and my children today and to position them throughout my house and around our property, our souls, and our bodies. I ask that angels protect my house from any intrusion and protect me and my family from any harmful demonic attacks, physical or mental.

I ask this prayer in the name of Jesus.

OUR IDENTITY IS SETTLED.

WE ARE SONS AND DAUGHTERS OF GOD, NOT SLAVES AND SERVANTS, BUT SONS AND DAUGHTERS WITH A SERVANT'S HEART!

Chapter 11

Be Wise, Evangelize

The fruit of the righteous is a tree of life,
And he who wins souls is wise.

Proverbs 11:30

The wise win souls! In this chapter, I want us to take a walk in the Spirit among the lampstands to get a closer look at who the torchbearers and keepers of the flame are in this moment and in this end-time move of the Spirit.

I've spoken to you in previous chapters about revival hubs arising, but there are many other places and ways God is moving in His power and His presence. Each one of them is different and unique, but the common denominator is Jesus in the midst of them. He is the focus of their attention.

Awaken to the Moment

For instance, God is moving on college campuses. There, it is prayer and intimacy more than preaching and noteworthy worship leaders. These leaders have no name and no face. Then there are the outreach centers where the rubber meets the road, feeding the hungry and working closely with the underprivileged in our communities. There are para-church organizations with an evangelistic purpose that are blooming and blossoming, preparing, participating, and partaking of the harvest right now.

There are nine modes and venues we want to visit on our journey so we can recognize and receive from them with faith, understanding, and expectation:

- Revival Hubs and Apostolic Centers
- College Campuses
- Outreach Centers
- Para-Church Organizations
- Online by Design
- Stadiums, Campaigns, and Crusades
- Street Evangelism
- Relational Evangelism
- Tent Meetings and Camp Meetings

Before we take this walk, let's look to our roots for a biblical basis, then the history of the early Church, and the work of the evangelist.

First, let's look at Proverbs 11:30 in context. Here it is with a verse before and a verse after:

> *He who troubles his own house will inherit the wind,*
> *And the fool will be servant to the wise of heart.*
> *The fruit of the righteous is a tree of life,*
> *And he who wins souls is wise.*
> *If the righteous will be recompensed on the earth,*
> *How much more the ungodly and the sinner.*
> Proverbs 11:29-31

Then we have Jesus' call for us to be fishers of men. In Matthew 4:19, He said:

> *Follow me and I will make you fishers of men.*

Interestingly enough, Jesus was not a fisherman Himself. He was a carpenter, and yet these fishermen left their nets and followed Him.

Let's look at verses 19-22 in the NIV to get the full picture of what was happening as Jesus was bringing His evangelistic team together:

Awaken to the Moment

"Come, follow me," Jesus said, "and I will send you out to fish for people."
At once they left their nets and followed him. Going on from there, he saw two other brothers, James son of Zebedee and his brother John. They were in a boat with their father Zebedee, preparing their nets. Jesus called them, and immediately they left the boat and their father and followed him. Matthew 4:19-22, NIV

As the Apostle Paul was building his team and commissioning and setting his disciple and spiritual son Timothy in place to pastor and lead the church Paul had birthed in the Spirit, he exhorted Timothy to do the work of an evangelist. Let's look at the full charge he gave his spiritual son:

"I charge you therefore before God and the Lord Jesus Christ, who will judge the living and the dead at His appearing and His kingdom: Preach the word! Be ready in season and out of season. Convince, rebuke, exhort, with all longsuffering and teaching. For the time will come when they will not endure sound doctrine, but according to their own desires, because they have itching

ears, they will heap up for themselves teachers; and they will turn their ears away from the truth, and be turned aside to fables. But you be watchful in all things, endure afflictions, do the work of an evangelist, fulfill your ministry."

2 Timothy 4:1-5

This is very powerful and speaks to conditions and obstacles we are facing today as church leaders. The parallels and paradigms are uncanny. This is how Paul perfectly described the end days and the present perilous times. Look closely, and you will see that we are in the last days. This is the eleventh hour, and we must awaken to the moment and come to the knowledge of the truth:

But know this, that in the last days perilous times will come: For men will be lovers of themselves, lovers of money, boasters, proud, blasphemers, disobedient to parents, unthankful, unholy, unloving, unforgiving, slanderers, without self-control, brutal, despisers of good, traitors, headstrong, haughty, lovers of pleasure rather than lovers of God, having a form of godliness but denying its power. And from such people turn away! For of this sort are those who creep into households and make captives of gullible women loaded down with sins, led away by various lusts, always learning and never able to come to the knowledge of the truth.

2 Timothy 3:1-7

We, too, must do the work of an evangelist and make full proof of our ministries. Timothy was a pastor and a teacher, but Paul exhorted him to do the work of an evangelist. All fivefold ministers, believers, and followers of Christ are called to testify and bear witness to the work of the living God, the Hope of Glory, in them. Lead others to the saving knowledge of Christ and make disciples … it is the mandate of the Messiah.

What is the work of an evangelist? The evangelist is to faithfully proclaim the Gospel of the Kingdom, the saving and healing Gospel of Jesus Christ, to make sinners aware of their sins, to correct with compassion, to encourage with hope, and to never lose hope in or begin to believe that man is beyond redemption.

Evangelists are not just itinerant ministers who have a microphone and a platform. Rather, they are someone with a burden for the lost, the wayward, and the backslider. They will have a heart for souls that beats and burns for the unsaved. In many cases, they have a biblical and spiritual burden to fill Heaven and rob Hell, and often they have a revelation of Hell that prompts them to be diligent to pursue the lost—even when it is a little uncomfortable.

We are all called to evangelize, but not all are called to the office gift of the evangelist, as laid out in Paul's writings:

> *And He Himself gave some to be apostles, some prophets, some evangelists, and some pastors and teachers, for the equipping of the saints for the work of ministry, for the edifying of the body of Christ.* Ephesians 4:11-12

In speaking and working with many fivefold evangelists, they share that they not only had a very real personal encounter with the Lord, but in many cases they had a very vivid revelation of Hell, and this put an urgency on their hearts. We know it is the Lord's desire that not one perish:

Awaken to the Moment

The Lord is not slack concerning His promise,
as some count slackness, but is longsuffering
toward us, not willing that any should perish
but that all should come to repentance.

2 Peter 3:9

I've had people say they don't have a burden for souls. My response is, "Stop the music! Get off the merry-go-round of life and seek the heart of the Father!" There is nothing deeper in the heart of God than His burden for lost souls, and His Word clearly tells us He is married to the backslider. This means that He will never forget the covenant commitment He made with them.

The primary ministry of the evangelist is to reconcile everything and every person to the Father. The truth is that God has given that mandate and ministry to every believer:

Now all things are of God, who has reconciled
us to Himself through Jesus Christ, and has
given us the ministry of reconciliation, that is,
that God was in Christ reconciling the world to
Himself, not imputing their trespasses to them,
and has committed to us the word of reconcilia-
tion. Now then, we are ambassadors for Christ,

as though God were pleading through us: we implore you on Christ's behalf, be reconciled to God. 2 Corinthians 5:18-20

We openly embrace the truth that we are ambassadors for Christ, so our viewpoint and priority order must be the same perspective as the One who sent us, and that is to reconcile everyone to God through Christ. As ambassadors, our perspective and priorities must be in alignment with His. As an ambassador, I don't have a right to override the policy of the One who delegated this authority or the luxury of my own opinion. I am representing the One who sent me. That is my role and my responsibility.

Most people are not won to Christ by a fancy televangelist; most are actually brought to faith by someone they are in relationship with and trust. Relational evangelism is by far the most effective way to build the Kingdom. When men and women hear and see the transforming power of the Gospel in the life of someone they know, it resonates with them. Sometimes that person shares their testimony, and at times the new believer becomes an eyewitness, and it begins a love chain of new life that spreads through a family or community and beyond.

There is a rejoicing that takes place in all of Heaven in the presence of angels when a sinner turns to God. Jesus clearly stated His heart in Luke 15 the Parable of the Lost Sheep:

> *Then all the tax collectors and the sinners drew near to Him to hear Him. And the Pharisees and scribes complained, saying, "This Man receives sinners and eats with them."*
>
> *So He spoke this parable to them, saying: "What man of you, having a hundred sheep, if he loses one of them, does not leave the ninety-nine in the wilderness, and go after the one which is lost until he finds it? And when he has found it, he lays it on his shoulders, rejoicing. And when he comes home, he calls together his friends and neighbors, saying to them, 'Rejoice with me, for I have found my sheep which was lost!' I say to you that likewise there will be more joy in heaven over one sinner who repents than over ninety-nine just persons who need no repentance."*   Luke 15:1-7

Other roles and responsibility of an evangelist, in addition to their primary function of personal soul-winner, are:

1. To be a part of a Local church, serving the vision of that fellowship and submitting their gifts, talents, and abilities, when reasonably possible, and at the request of leadership to serve on the fivefold pastoral team. To minister is to serve.

2. Traveling itinerate ministry, preaching the Gospel of Kingdom in local churches, the marketplace, and in crusades live, or in other venues such as multi-media and social-media outlets.

3. Impart, empower, and equip others in their gift and calling. Disciple and mentor, raising up sons and daughters, including other evangelists, with a servant's heart.

4. Establish and participate in evangelism and outreach endeavors with the purpose of extending the Kingdom and building the local church.

5. Foreign and domestic mission assignments and trips.

6. Prophetic evangelism directed by dreams, visions, revelation knowledge, and/or divine insight and strategies, to present the Good News to individuals, groups, cities, or nations for divine appointments and destiny encounters with the intent to lead people to Christ.

Note: Many times, as an evangelist preaches the Gospel, there are signs, wonders, miracles, deliverances, baptisms in water and in the Spirit that accompany and confirm the Word:

> *God also bearing them witness, both with signs and wonders, and with divers miracles, and gifts of the Holy Ghost, according to his own will?* Hebrews 2:4, KJV

Here are some biblical examples of the work of the evangelist in action:

The woman at the well: She received Christ through a word of knowledge concerning her marital status. Also, she received a word of wisdom on how the Lord would raise up a people who would worship Him in Spirit and truth. Then Jesus revealed His true identity as Messiah to her. She received Him as Lord through faith and then evangelized and led others to Him.

The woman at the tomb on Resurrection Sunday: She came back rejoicing to testify that the tomb was empty and that Jesus was alive.

Philip the evangelist in Acts 8: He preached the Gospel with demonstrations of power—signs, wonders, miracles and the gifts of the Spirit—seeing salvations, deliverances and baptisms in water and in the Holy Spirit. Later he was found greeting and hosting Paul and his party in Acts 21, serving as an elder/leader in the local church in Caesarea:

> *On the next day we who were Paul's companions departed and came to Caesarea, and entered the house of Philip the evangelist, who was one of the seven, and stayed with him. Now this man had four virgin daughters who prophesied.*

And as we stayed many days, a certain prophet named Agabus came down from Judea. When he had come to us, he took Paul's belt, bound his own hands and feet, and said, "Thus says the Holy Spirit, 'So shall the Jews at Jerusalem bind the man who owns this belt, and deliver him into the hands of the Gentiles.' "

Now when we heard these things, both we and those from that place pleaded with him not to go up to Jerusalem. Then Paul answered, "What do you mean by weeping and breaking my heart? For I am ready not only to be bound, but also to die at Jerusalem for the name of the Lord Jesus." So when he would not be persuaded, we ceased, saying, "The will of the Lord be done."

Acts 21:8-14

Peter in Acts 10 at the house of Cornelius: There were household salvations and baptisms in the Spirit with speaking in tongues, a sign of the impartation of the gift.

Paul and Barnabas in Acts 11: They were set apart and launched out on a mission assignment and journey.

As they ministered to the Lord and fasted, the Holy Spirit said, "Now separate to Me Barnabas and Saul for the work to which I have called them." Then, having fasted and prayed, and laid hands on them, they sent them away.

Acts 13:2-3

The Apostle Paul in Acts 19: He was evangelizing in Ephesus with demonstrations of the power of the Spirit, signs, wonders, and miracles, and baptisms of the Spirit. There was a powerful release of the anointing that brought such great conviction that the people purged their homes of items of idolatry, witchcraft, and divination. Then they burned these items as a sign and demonstration of the fruit of their repentance.

Be wise, evangelize. We must *Awaken to the Moment*, for the harvest is all around us, ready to be reaped. This is a *Kingdom Reality*.

PRAYER:

Heavenly Father, thank You for the harvest. You are the Lord of the Harvest, and we are children of the harvest. Thank You for giving us a heart after Your own heart, a heart for souls, a burden for the wounded, the broken, the lost, and the wayward, a burning desire that not one would perish but all would come to the knowledge of You and Your love. Thank You for wisdom that we may discern the urgency of the moment. Thank You for perfect timing. Thank You for preparing our hearts and the hearts of those we will encounter today. Thank You for divine appointments, destiny encounters, and for the words to speak in season and out, as You teach us to be fishers of men.

In Jesus' mighty name, I release over my brothers a fresh anointing of boldness to declare Your goodness and to be witnesses of what You have done in our lives and of the fact that You live in our hearts, that our God lives.

Amen!

THERE IS NOTHING DEEPER IN THE HEART OF GOD THAN HIS BURDEN FOR LOST SOULS, AND HIS WORD CLEARLY TELLS US HE IS MARRIED TO THE BACKSLIDER!

Chapter 12

Preparing for Harvest

Do you not say, "There are yet four months, then comes the harvest"? Look, I tell you, lift up your eyes, and see that the fields are white for harvest."   John 4:35

These are indeed days of harvest, and we need to have the eyes of our understanding opened and awakened to the moment. Let us arise and reap.

The enemy would like nothing more than for you and me to miss this tremendous moment in time, our day of visitation. He wants us to think it's still far off. He says, "Oh yeah, it's coming, but you have time. Don't worry about it. There's no need to be intense. Take it easy. Enjoy yourself. Everything's going to be okay."

Awaken to the Moment

You simply must recognize that voice, or it will rob you of your harvest and steal your destiny.

Now is the time. Let us grow together, go together, and sow together. Let us partner in the harvest right here and right now. It is everywhere around us. The hearts of many have been prepared by the difficult season of Covid and the trials and tribulations related to the last five to seven years of battle, as well as all the distractions of the moment and the fantasyland mentality that Hollywood and the rest of the media and the entertainment industry have heaped upon us.

Fortunately, a sense of true reality has now begun to stir in many. We are about to see the defining line more clearly, as the huge gap begins to get wider and wider. We are about to experience the Parable of the Wheat and Tares Jesus described in Matthew 13 played out. We need wisdom to watch, wait, look and listen so that we don't miss the harvest the Lord has prepared for us to reap in this moment. We don't know the hearts of men, and we must give Him the opportunity to weigh them.

Preparing for Harvest

But when the grain had sprouted and produced a crop, then the tares also appeared. So the servants of the owner came and said to him, "Sir, did you not sow good seed in your field? How then does it have tares?"

He said to them, "An enemy has done this."

The servants said to him, "Do you want us then to go and gather them up?"

But he said, "No, lest while you gather up the tares you also uproot the wheat with them. Let both grow together until the harvest, and at the time of harvest I will say to the reapers, 'First gather together the tares and bind them in bundles to burn them, but gather the wheat into my barn.'"   Matthew 13:26-30

Paul spoke of that same process in Galatians 6:

Let both grow together until the harvest, and at harvest time I will tell the reapers, "Gather the weeds first and bind them in bundles to be burned, but gather the wheat into my barn."
Galatians 6:9, ESV

One recent evening, while I was sharing about the harvest with some partners on Zoom, the

Lord dropped a word of wisdom into my heart. Some individuals under the influence of a religious spirit will try to keep us from sharing our powerful testimonies by making us think that doing so is boastful and prideful. It can be … if we're not giving the glory to God. By not sharing, however, we lose the great power of our testimony of what Christ has done in us and through us and what we've seen Him do in others. We overcome by the blood of the Lamb AND the word of our testimony (see Revelation 12:11).

Paul spoke of this and plainly described and explained the difference and encouraged us to *"boast in the Lord"*:

> *So that no one may boast before him. It is because of him that you are in Christ Jesus, who has become for us wisdom from God—that is, our righteousness, holiness and redemption. Therefore, as it is written: "Let the one who boasts boast in the Lord."*
>
> 1 Corinthians 1:29-31, NIV

When we testify or share the miracles we've seen and heard, it raises the faith level in those who hear it. Why? Because faith comes by hearing. When their faith level rises, they are better able to believe and receive their own miracle. Therefore, let us declare boldly what the Lord has done and not allow the enemy to rob us and others of the blessings and miracles He has for them.

We need to take advantage of the opportunities presented to us to share with others the tangible love and goodness of God. Relational or one-on-one evangelism is the most effective method. Each of us should write our testimony down, know it well and understand how to present it when the moment arises. This is part of what Paul meant when he wrote:

Study to shew thyself approved unto God, a workman that needeth not to be ashamed, rightly dividing the word of truth.
2 Timothy 2:15, KJV

I leave my personal testimony card with many people who I get a moment to meet and share with as a point of contact as I travel. Not only does our original testimony have power, but so do the testimonies from each victory of our walk with Christ, both in the small and the large. There is power in our testimonies of God's constant goodness. Whether it is healing, financial blessing, or deliverance, let's share it and give glory and thanksgiving to God for all He has done. In this way we can add "whosoevers" to the Kingdom.

The Lord kisses our testimonies and anoints our words to open and prepare the hearts of the hearer. It is the anointing on those words that breaks the yoke and opens the eyes of the understanding of the hearer.

Yes, sometimes we have stepped out, and it didn't seem to bear fruit or work out. But we cannot let that stop us from pressing in again. Our part is to testify. The rest is up to God.

In some cases, it takes multiple attempts. Those who hear us are not rejecting us. They just may not be quite ready. Go ahead and share, sow the seed or sprinkle a little more water on the seed someone else has sown. God will do the changing and bring the increase.

We can't save anyone, but let's just do our part, sowing the seed and watering it in prayer. Then leave the rest to the Hound of Heaven, the Lover of Our Souls, the Holy Spirit.

And never give up. The Word says:

> *And let us not be weary in well doing: for in due season we shall reap, if we faint not.*
>
> Galatians 6:9, KJV

We shall reap … if we don't faint. There must be an urgency in our spirits for souls, and if we are to be effective fishers of men, we must stay balanced, waiting on the Lord and His timing. Since He is the Lord of the harvest, we must let Him lead and guide us. James wrote:

> *Be patient, therefore, brothers, until the coming of the Lord. See how the farmer waits for the precious fruit of the earth, being patient about it, until it receives the early and the late rains.*
>
> James 5:7, ESV

We need to be diligent, persistent, strategic, and consistent and take advantage of as many opportunities as we can. Sow into the harvest bountifully and leave the rest to the Lord of the Harvest.

The Word speaks very clearly about the sluggard, or lazy man, in the harvest season:

Awaken to the Moment

Sluggards do not plow in season;
  so at harvest time they look but find nothing.
                                    Proverbs 20:4, NIV

If we wait for the perfect moment, we won't sow at all. The Word gives us wisdom about the diligent and the sluggard:

> *He becometh poor that dealeth with a slack hand: but the hand of the diligent maketh rich. He that gathereth in summer is a wise son: but he that sleepeth in harvest is a son that causeth shame.* Proverbs 10:4-5, KJV

Let me share here five basic and practical keys to start you off. As you attempt to put them into practice, don't allow fear or guilt to stop you. Be bold, but not loud or rude:

1. Stop, look and listen! Be observant and aware. Expect God to guide your steps and arrange divine encounters. When they happen, take advantage of them. If you are faithful in a little, He will surely give you more.

2. Write your testimonies down, then read and study them. This is not to embellish and enhance them. It gives you an opportunity to be more thankful in your prayer life. Build a spiritual monument around that testimony in your heart.

3. Try to act somewhat normal and enthusiastic. Be kind, thoughtful, cheerful, and display good manners that would support your testimony and not hinder it. Show the same respect you would expect of someone else.

4. Don't Christianize, don't beat them over the head with your Bible or try to display your Bible knowledge or superiority.

5. Don't forget to pull in the net if you have something in it. Don't be afraid to ask the questions that need to be answered.

As you converse, ask pertinent questions. Is this person a believer in Jesus? Do they know Him as Lord and Savior? If something were to happen to them right now, are they sure they would go to Heaven? Do they have the blessed assurance that they are saved? etc.

Time is running out. As John declared:

> *And the Spirit and the bride say, "Come!"*
> *And let him who hears say, "Come!"*
> *And let him who thirsts come.*
> *Whoever desires, let him take the water of life*
> *freely.*   Revelation 22:17

In closing this chapter, here is a prophetic poem written by Pastor Mave Moyer on April 28, 2023, during one of our Partners Appreciation Zoom Nights for Eagle Worldwide Ministries:

> *The waters of life are flowing afresh...*
> *No price demanded of me and of you...*
> *Our Savior has come...redemption is sure...*
> *He's done what He only could do.*
>
> *Come to the water...bring others...*
> *His mercy is here...new today...*
> *Forgiveness is waiting...grace still abides...*
> *His power has not passed away.*

Preparing for Harvest

Do not delay... the time is at hand...
The harvest is white in the field...
Take up your sickle...step into place...
To His Spirit...we must bend and yield.

Now is the time for reaping...
These are the days of God's BEST...
This season shall bring great abundance...
The children of God will be blessed.

Heaven is preparing to shower...
His love down…all over the earth...
As we rise together ... one voice for Him...
And declare His matchless worth.

Time to put on...the Lord Jesus…
Time to arise and shine...
Time to get it together...
Time for us to align.

Our faithfulness shall be rewarded...
More than enough is on the way...
As our hearts fully surrender...
And we answer the call to pray.

Awaken to the Moment

NOW is the day of visitation...
Hungry hearts are ignited anew...
God is coming in power...
He's coming for me and for you.

And as the world grows darker...
Our light will shine ever more...
His Spirit in us shall be evident...
As His truth and His grace is outpoured.

Now is the day of His Kingdom...
His purpose and will shall be done...
His glory shall cover all of the earth...
And we shall shine with the light of His Son.

Yes, we must *Awaken to the Moment*, for the harvest is all around us, ready to be reaped. This is a *Kingdom Reality*.

Prayer:

Heavenly Father, I thank You for those who are called to this end-time harvest, to do the work of evangelism, to extend and advance Your Kingdom. I ask that by the power of Your Spirit, You would release a fresh anointing, fresh fire, a fresh burden on our hearts for souls, that by Your Spirit, You would teach us to be fishers of men, that You would give us wisdom to win souls, that You would guide us, direct us, and protect us by Your Spirit.

I declare over you today divine appointments, a holy boldness, destiny encounters with the lost, the wounded, the wayward, the backsliders, and the prodigals, that you would bear fruit and fruit that lasts.

In the glorious name of Christ Jesus,
our Lord,
our Savior,
our Messiah.

THE ENEMY WOULD LIKE NOTHING MORE THAN FOR YOU AND ME TO MISS THIS TREMENDOUS MOMENT IN TIME, OUR DAY OF VISITATION. HE WANTS US TO THINK IT'S STILL FAR OFF!

Chapter 13

The Battle for Balance

My people are destroyed for lack of knowledge: because thou hast rejected knowledge, I will also reject thee, that thou shalt be no priest to me: seeing thou hast forgotten the law of thy God, I will also forget thy children.

Hosea 4:6, KJV

In this prophetic season of Kingdom reset, we have been transitioning through and into this new moment. We are entering into an even greater season of change, transition, and transformation, one that will require us to take a realistic look at ourselves, our purpose, our plans, our priorities, our mode of operation, and, most importantly, our motives. There is a battle raging in each one of our hearts, in each one of our lives, in our families, our communities, and our nations, a battle of good and evil. These are days of war and roses. The battles are real, and so is spiritual warfare.

The Bible tells us in Hosea: *"My people are destroyed from lack of knowledge"* (Hosea 4:6). There is a battle raging in our minds, in our hearts, and in our lives, a battle for our time, energy, and attention. The Kingdom reality of our life in Christ is not all that simple at this *kairos* moment in time.

In this journey, we are bombarded with opportunity, distraction, and a flood of information, and voices are being unleashed on us from every side. The media and powerful forces of seduction in advertising are manipulating and controlling us and our children. Forces are at work, influencing our choices, along with peer pressure and bullying, not just some kid in school, but organized, planned, and sophisticated forces of darkness and evil trying to abort our rights to free speech, freedom of religion, and even the freedom to think differently and independently of the *status quo*.

The cancel culture in our society is trying to marginalize, intimidate, and silence us in order to control us. But our God is not a cookie-cutter God. He is a personal and relational God, a God of individuality and creativity. We are all made in His likeness, yet we are individuals with unique personalities. He gave us free will that He Himself will never take from us, so we need to be careful that we don't just give it away by allowing others to take it from us. We must be bold and courageous and stand for freedom, or it will be taken from us. We must take a stand, not only for our own freedom, but also for our children and our children's children.

There is a cry on the heart of God for Freedom now, in this moment … if you have ears to hear and eyes to see what the Spirit is saying to the Church. We need to discern the voice, wisdom, and purpose of God in our lives, so that we choose the right door and the right course of action in the appropriate and perfect timing (God's timing).

The Lord is trying to bring Kingdom balance and structure to us in this season and hour, so the harvest He is sending will be properly stewarded. He has made His will clear: that we would bear fruit and fruit that lasts.

Many of us have experienced a season of great pruning, not because we necessarily did something wrong, but the good intent and Kingdom vision of God for us in the pruning process is that we would bear more fruit in this final harvest. He is pruning the dead and wild branches and building structure so that we will bud, bloom, blossom, and bear more fruit.

The first foundational truth of the Kingdom prepares us for this moment. It can be found in the greatest sermon ever preached, the Sermon on the Mount. Let's look at it again:

> *But seek first his kingdom and his righteous-*
> *ness, and all these things will be given to you*
> *as well.* Matthew 6:33, NIV

God is also at work in us to restore proper Kingdom priority order in our lives. He is show-ing us the wisdom and benefit of balance. My wife, Mave, says, "Every mile of road has two miles of ditch." We, the Church, all too often find ourselves in one ditch or the other.

Proverbs tells us:

> *Honest scales and balances belong to the LORD;*
> *all the weights in the bag are of his making.*
> Proverbs 16:11, NIV

I recently shared one of the "Minute with Maxwell"[1] devotionals with two of my online mentoring groups. It was called "The Screaming Eagles" and "The Pensacola Band of Brothers." John Maxwell had such great things to say, like "Activity doesn't always equal accomplishment." Maxwell suggests:

- When you list the things you need to do, put them in the order of priority, with the most important first.
- Set important meetings and functions in the sweet spot of your day, those times where you are stronger and on your game.
- If you can only can two things today, then do two of the "biggies."
- Be time sensitive.

Let's put these ideas into action. I'm sure they will produce better results.

Not long ago, I spoke on Balance and Priority on "The Prophetic Edge," my Wednesday Facebook Live on the Russ and Mave Moyer page. We need to operate in faith, function, and focus if we're going to have maximum impact.

---

1. https://johnmaxwell.podbean.com

We need to concentrate our energy and invest our time wisely.

When I'm working with and mentoring young leaders, I want to help them channel and harness their positive energy without losing their zeal. We, as believers, followers of Christ, must be zealous in our walk and pursuit. We must live our lives with a passion for Christ and compassion for His people. At the same time, there needs to be a balance in our lives of family, recreation, career, entertainment, and time set aside for prayer, meditation, ongoing education, and personal self-improvement.

Christians must avoid being like enthusiastic Israel. Paul said that they had zeal without knowledge (see Titus 2:11-13). Zeal is defined by the Oxford Online Dictionary as "great energy or enthusiasm in pursuit of a cause or an objective."[2] Christians must be zealous (see Titus 2:14), but as with any part of our Christianity and our lives, there has to be a balance. Zeal without knowledge can be a dangerous thing:

---

2. https://www.oed.com

The Battle for Balance

For the grace of God has appeared that offers
salvation to all people. It teaches us to say "No"
to ungodliness and worldly passions, and to
live self-controlled, upright and godly lives in
this present age, while we wait for the blessed
hope—the appearing of the glory of our great
God and Savior, Jesus Christ.

Titus 2:11-13, NIV

Some days I can't be sure whether this a bal-
ancing act or a juggling act. Again, every mile
of road has two miles of ditch. God is weeding
and seeding our gardens. He is preparing and
training us to rule and reign, to overcome and
to live a victorious and an abundant Kingdom
life in Christ. We must do our part:

Therefore let them give us two bulls; and let
them choose one bull for themselves, cut it in
pieces, and lay it on the wood, but put no fire
under it; and I will prepare the other bull, and
lay it on the wood, but put no fire under it.

1 Kings 18:23

We hear some talk about pastors and leaders suffering from burnout, and it's very real.

However, I've seen people who waste a lot of time, energy, and effort because of a lack of balance, personal discipline, organizational skills, and wrong order of priorities in their lives. I've also seen people who lack relational skills and any sense of reality and feel they only need a three-day work week and four days rest and, of course, top, full-time pay and benefits. This shows a sense and spirit of entitlement, when we know God worked six days and rested one.

As I said, pastoral burnout is real, and the role of a pastor has been wrongly defined and given unrealistic expectations. One person is just not able to be everything to everyone, and so the concept of team ministry, apostolic five-fold firefight teams, with each office gift operating in healthy relationship and respect for the call and gift of God on one another, is sorely needed today.

A congregation of believers must no longer be strangers but fellow citizens of the household, understanding their identity as sons and daughters, the priesthood of believers partnering together to get things done—rebuilding the walls, re-digging old wells of refreshing and revival, and building and advancing the Kingdom of God through the local church. In this way, we can impact our communities and transform our society by demonstrating Kingdom life and reality, with men and women of integrity, character, and honor letting the love and light of Jesus Christ change our society one life at a time.

Yes, we need to know the facts and stats of professionals like the Barna Group, who have their finger on the facts of the Christian church community today, but we must also walk in faith, not in fear, knowing that the anointing of God, His favor, His truth and the Spirit of God can trump the facts.

We need to pray for our pastors, leaders, and their families in this difficult prophetic and strategic moment. We need wisdom, and we need mature leadership that will guide this generation to a victorious Kingdom lifestyle. I declare and decree that God's royal priesthood will rise to the occasion, in unity—one heart, one spirit, with generations and streams flowing together as one.

May the tribe of Hungry cry out for more of the Lord, so that Malachi 4 will be fulfilled in this season:

Awaken to the Moment

"For behold, the day is coming,
Burning like an oven,
And all the proud, yes, all who do wickedly will
be stubble.
And the day which is coming shall burn them
up,"
Says the LORD of hosts,
"That will leave them neither root nor branch.
But to you who fear My name
The Sun of Righteousness shall arise
With healing in His wings;
And you shall go out
And grow fat like stall-fed calves.
You shall trample the wicked,
For they shall be ashes under the soles of your
feet
On the day that I do this,"
Says the LORD of hosts.

"Remember the Law of Moses, My servant,
Which I commanded him in Horeb for all Israel,
With the statutes and judgments.
Behold, I will send you Elijah the prophet
Before the coming of the great and dreadful day
of the LORD.
And he will turn

The Battle for Balance

The hearts of the fathers to the children,
And the hearts of the children to their fathers,
Lest I come and strike the earth with a curse.
Malachi 4:1-6

These are the last days, and the restoration of all things will highlight and fulfill Isaiah 2:2-3:

Now it shall come to pass in the latter days
That the mountain of the LORD's house
Shall be established on the top of the mountains,
And shall be exalted above the hills;
And all nations shall flow to it.
Many people shall come and say,
"Come, and let us go up to the mountain of
the LORD,
To the house of the God of Jacob;
He will teach us His ways,
And we shall walk in His paths."
For out of Zion shall go forth the law,
And the word of the LORD from Jerusalem."

Yes, we must *Awaken to the Moment* and find the proper balance. This is a *Kingdom Reality*.

PRAYER:

Father, we come together in unity, praying for pastors, leaders, missionaries, itinerant ministers, marketplace ministers, and their families. In this season, may Your hand of favor, blessing, and love rest upon them. Guide them and direct them with the power of Your Spirit. Bless them with revelation, wisdom, and understanding. Bless them with Your peace. Refresh them in this moment. Give them hope, healing, energy, vision, and strength to finish their race and leave a legacy that will live on long after they are gone.

I pray in glorious name of Jesus!
Amen!

THE LORD IS TRYING TO BRING KINGDOM BALANCE AND STRUCTURE TO US IN THIS SEASON AND HOUR, SO THE HARVEST HE IS SENDING WILL BE PROPERLY STEWARDED!

Chapter 14

Is This a Dress Rehearsal or the Opening Act?

"Then you shall see and become radiant,
And your heart shall swell with joy;
Because the abundance of the sea shall be turned
to you,
The wealth of the Gentiles shall come to you.
The multitude of camels shall cover your land,
The dromedaries of Midian and Ephah;
All those from Sheba shall come;
They shall bring gold and incense,
And they shall proclaim the praises of the LORD.
All the flocks of Kedar shall be gathered together
to you,
The rams of Nebaioth shall minister to you;
They shall ascend with acceptance on My altar,
And I will glorify the house of My glory.

Awaken to the Moment

"Who are these who fly like a cloud,
And like doves to their roosts?
Surely the coastlands shall wait for Me;
And the ships of Tarshish will come first,
To bring your sons from afar,
Their silver and their gold with them,
To the name of the LORD your God,
And to the Holy One of Israel,
Because He has glorified you.

"The sons of foreigners shall build up your
walls,
And their kings shall minister to you;
For in My wrath I struck you,
But in My favor I have had mercy on you.
Therefore your gates shall be open continually;
They shall not be shut day or night,
That men may bring to you the wealth of the
Gentiles,
And their kings in procession.
For the nation and kingdom which will not
serve you shall perish,
And those nations shall be utterly ruined."

Isaiah 60:5-12

I personally believe the Lord is raising the platform, raising our level of expectation, and opening the curtain to reveal to us a new dimension of Kingdom reality. He is ready to reveal to the world what they are earnestly awaiting—the manifestation of His true sons and daughters.

A new breed of leader is coming over the hill. They have no name, no face, and no agenda but God's. They are dedicated to His service and committed to His purpose and to the call on their lives. They are ready to pick up their cross and follow after Him with reckless abandonment, fully consecrating themselves to Him, while setting themselves in total opposition to the idols of this world. They have a zeal for His House, a spirit of worship and oneness, and are operating in true unity, demonstrating and bearing witness to His deity in their lives by their love for Him and one another.

Let's you and I take a Kingdom reality look at what the Church is embarking on in this amazing moment. As we make this final turn and head down the home stretch, fixed on finishing well, let's press into the wire for the great victory that you and I and our generation were born and ordained for from the very beginning of time.

As we awaken, we will have eyes to see and ears to hear what the Spirit is saying to the Church. We will become keenly aware of our present situation, as spiritual discernment and wisdom will be released to fully recognize the season we are in and the spirits that are operating for and against us.

This situation and season will be birthed out of intimacy with the Lord, and the remnant will begin to come forth from different streams and flow together in true unity. Isaiah 60 will be fulfilled before our eyes.

Yes, we are going to see, hear, and appear as the sons and daughters of God as foretold in Romans. Yes, a great harvest will come to us from the highways and byways: the lost, the prodigals, Israel, and the backslidden and wayward Church, lost in its religion, culture, and tradition.

Yes, they will come and bless the remnant as the transference of the wealth of the wicked will come into our hands to fund the end-time harvest and end-time ministries to advance the Kingdom of God.

Yes, the camels are coming, bringing the provision for the vision, the blessings of the nations. We shall be planted by the river of life and be refreshed, revived, and restored. We shall begin to bear fruit and fruit that lasts in every season, answering the Great Commission, making disciples, and sons and daughters who will walk in Jesus' footsteps and worship Him in Spirit and truth, while preaching the Gospel of the Kingdom and demonstrating His power with an understanding of His presence and glory. They will live in the Spirit and be led by the Spirit.

We shall awaken and arise and shine to fulfill the Messiah Mandate of Isaiah 61, but first things first:

> *Arise, shine;*
> *For your light has come!*
> *And the glory of the LORD is risen upon you.*
> *For behold, the darkness shall cover the earth,*
> *And deep darkness the people;*
> *But the LORD will arise over you,*
> *And His glory will be seen upon you.*
> *The Gentiles shall come to your light,*
> *And kings to the brightness of your rising.*

Awaken to the Moment

Lift up your eyes all around, and see:
They all gather together, they come to you;
Your sons shall come from afar,
And your daughters shall be nursed at your side. Isaiah 60:1-4

When we have come into the fullness of time, we will see and experience restoration and reconciliation. It will come upon us suddenly, personally, as well as in our families, churches, cities, and nations.

This is a NOW moment, and there is an Elijah cry on the heart of God that will release a sound in the Earth that will separate the sheep from the goats, the wheat from the tares. That sound will gather and scatter as God weighs the hearts of men and nations.

We are about to step into our place of proper apostolic alignment, to be prepared, empowered, equipped, and launched into our destiny, fulfilling every word spoken and every promise made by Jesus, our Messiah, our King, our Lord, our Savior, our Healer, and our Deliverer.

He is the King of Glory, who will lead His end-time army into battle. He is coming riding on a white horse with fire in His eyes and a scepter in His hand, as described by John the Beloved in Revelation:

> *Now I saw heaven opened, and behold, a white horse. And He who sat on him was called Faithful and True, and in righteousness He judges and makes war. His eyes were like a flame of fire, and on His head were many crowns. He had a name written that no one knew except Himself. He was clothed with a robe dipped in blood, and His name is called The Word of God. And the armies in heaven, clothed in fine linen, white and clean, followed Him on white horses. Now out of His mouth goes a sharp sword, that with it He should strike the nations. And He Himself will rule them with a rod of iron. He Himself treads the winepress of the fierceness and wrath of Almighty God. And He has on His robe and on His thigh a name written:*
> *KING OF KINGS AND LORD OF LORDS."*
> Revelation 19:11-16

He is also the Good Shepherd, with the heart of the Father, and He will heal and restore His Family, His Church. He is also the Bridegroom, coming to fulfill His covenant promise for His

Awaken to the Moment

Bride, who is even now being made ready in this season. She is a bride without spot or wrinkle, and this will not just be a visitation, but, rather, a holy habitation. He will adorn Her with His presence, and her light will shine as Isaiah foretold.

His Bride will be anointed with the double blessing to fulfill Her mandate and divine destiny. This generation is marked for destiny and purpose to usher in the Second Coming of the Lord:

> *The Spirit of the LORD God is upon Me,*
> *Because the LORD has anointed Me*
> *To preach good tidings to the poor;*
> *He has sent Me to heal the brokenhearted,*
> *To proclaim liberty to the captives,*
> *And to open the prison to those who are bound;*
> *To proclaim the acceptable year of the LORD,*
> *And the day of vengeance of our God;*
> *To comfort all who mourn,*
> *To console those who mourn in Zion,*
> *To give them beauty for ashes,*
> *The oil of joy for mourning,*
> *The garment of praise for the spirit of heaviness;*
> *That they may be called trees of righteousness,*

The planting of the L*ORD*, *that He may be glorified.*

"And they shall rebuild the old ruins,
They shall raise up the former desolations,
And they shall repair the ruined cities,
The desolations of many generations.
Strangers shall stand and feed your flocks,
And the sons of the foreigner
Shall be your plowmen and your vinedressers.
But you shall be named the priests of the L*ORD*,
They shall call you the servants of our God.
You shall eat the riches of the Gentiles,
And in their glory you shall boast.
Instead of your shame you shall have double honor,
And instead of confusion they shall rejoice in their portion.
Therefore in their land they shall possess double;
Everlasting joy shall be theirs."

Isaiah 61:1-7

The victory is near at hand, closer and sooner then we know. The kingdoms of this world will become the kingdoms of our God. We are about to enter a new dimension of Kingdom reality.

Awaken to the Moment

This isn't a sad rescue mission; this is the victory ride of the called, the chosen, and the faithful (see Revelation 17:14).

Yes, we must *Awaken to the Moment*, for the curtain is rising. This is a *Kingdom Reality*.

PRAYER:

My prayer for you, as we close this chapter, is that you would fully come to a place of intimacy with the Lord, and He would help you turn the page, so that you can step into this new season full of hope, faith, and expectation, that you would awaken to this new and exciting moment in the Spirit, that you would walk in a brand new dimension of Kingdom reality. May the Lord bless you and keep you in this precious moment in time.

I declare and decree over you and your family a fresh anointing, a fresh stirring of hunger, and a thirst for God's presence. I release a fresh anointing over your life for fulfilment of His destiny purpose and plan for your life. May the blessing, the light, and the love of the Lord rest upon you in a powerful way, that, according to His Word and promise, He would light your path and guide your steps, that not one seed would fall to the ground, but that you would reap the fullness of the harvest He intended for you. God bless you and may you and your family serve the Lord all the days of your life. In Jesus' mighty name I pray!

A NEW BREED OF LEADER IS COMING OVER THE HILL. THEY HAVE NO NAME, NO FACE, AND NO AGENDA BUT GOD'S!

Chapter 15

Fighting for Revival, Not Survival

There shall come forth a Rod from the stem of Jesse,
And a Branch shall grow out of his roots.
The Spirit of the LORD shall rest upon Him,
The Spirit of wisdom and understanding,
The Spirit of counsel and might,
The Spirit of knowledge and of the fear of the
LORD.   Isaiah 11:1-2

In the midst of the battle, the lines can sometimes become quite blurry. As the sayings go,
"You can't see the forest for the trees," and "You
don't know the players without a scorecard." In
this moment, more than ever, we need discernment and wisdom from the Lord, along with the
Spirit of might. We need the promise of Isaiah
11:1-2 to come upon the Body of Christ.

Awaken to the Moment

We need a fresh Pentecost, a fresh anointing, fresh fire to fall upon us. We need to look at things with a Kingdom vision, meaning through the eyes and the heart of the King, not in the natural perspective, but with spiritual insight from the very heart of God.

These are the days of war and roses, and we need to be prepared for battle. We must make sure we identify the targets and objectives of the battle. This is just as important as knowing the weapons of our warfare and the rules of engagement. We need to keep our eye on the ball and not be distracted or deceived, and we cannot settle for less than the best God has for us. This is about revival, not survival.

Jesus came that we may have life and have it abundantly. He wants us to be blessed and to prosper in every way ... as our soul prospers. For our part, we need to bind our minds to the mind of Christ. We need to walk in revival and press into the heart of God for a move of His Spirit. We also may need to change our mode of operation, our techniques, tactics, and strategies, to reach this generation where they are. But, let's not change the overcoming victorious message, mission, or mandate of the King of Glory.

The good news is that Christ lives in the hearts and lives of His people. He is who He says He is, and He can and will do everything He said He will do. There is no other way to the Father but through the Son.

Jesus said in John 14:6:

I am the way, the truth, and the life. No one comes to the Father except through Me.

There is no other way to the Father, no other way to God, no other name to call but the name that is above every other name in Heaven and Earth, the name of Jesus.

You and I need to change gears right now. We must grab hold of the moment and fight the good fight of faith. This is the time to apply our faith and put it into action, with boots on the ground, taking territory for the King and His Kingdom. We need to release the Spirit of life, the Spirit of revival. I'm not looking for some man or woman who will bring us revival; I'm looking for the God of Revival.

In the meantime, I must not walk in fear or have any obligation to any man but to love him. What God desires is for us to raise up a prophetic army, a prophetic generation. That includes every single one of us, and He wants us to declare victory in His name over this generation and over every tribe, every tongue, and every nation with healing and hope.

We must awaken now in this moment. It's time to come back to God, to partner with Him, to bring refreshing, revival, and restoration to His Church, His Bride. It's time to come back to church, come back to our spiritual roots and fulfill our destiny in Christ the King. It's time to raise our level of expectation and come into agreement with the Word and the Spirit of God, time to grab hold of the horns of the altar and cry, "His Will be done, His Kingdom come, here and now, on Earth as it is in Heaven." It's time to walk and live in the Spirit and allow the Spirit to lead us to the greatest victory, the greatest moment in history. Let Him lead us to the victory He won for us. It's time to lift our heads and cry out, "Maranatha! Come, Lord Jesus! Come quickly!"

If, somewhere in this book, you have realized in your walk or journey in life, you've wandered away from God, listen now to His heart cry, and come home to Him. This is the moment to come to Him. Return to Him with all your heart and all your might, with all you are and all you ever hope to be. He loves you beyond anything you can imagine, explain, or comprehend with your natural mind. He is crying and calling out, deep crying out to deep, heart to heart, and Spirit to spirit.

Maybe you've been in church your whole life, and you know all about Jesus, but you don't really "know" Him. You don't have a real relationship with Him the way I've described;, a walking, talking, living relationship with a living and loving God and Father. This is that moment ordained for you from the beginning of time. It starts all over again, brand-new, right here and right now. *"Whoever calls upon the name of the Lord shall be saved,"* and I declare this is the acceptable day of the Lord for you.

Paul wrote in Romans 10:8-13:

> *But what does it say?"The word is near you, in your mouth and in your heart" (that is, the word of faith which we preach): that if you confess with your mouth the Lord Jesus and believe in your heart that God has raised Him from the dead, you will be saved. For with the*

heart one believes unto righteousness, and with the mouth confession is made unto salvation. For the Scripture says, "Whoever believes on Him will not be put to shame." For there is no distinction between Jew and Greek, for the same Lord over all is rich to all who call upon Him. For "whoever calls on the name of the Lord shall be saved."

My friend, you and I must *Awaken to the Moment,* for this is the day of salvation. This is a definite *Kingdom Reality.*

Pray this prayer with me now:

Lord Jesus, thank You for loving me enough to speak to me about the condition of my heart and the sin in my life. I confess that You, Jesus, are the Son of God, my Savior, and my Lord, that You died on the cross for me and for my sin, that the Father raised You from the dead, and You live. I ask You to forgive me of my sin, and I am sorry for anything I've done to hurt You, to hurt others, or to hurt myself. I receive You into my heart today, Jesus, afresh and

anew. Come into my heart! Come into my life! Come and live Your life, Jesus, through me!

Amen!

If you just prayed this prayer with me, meant it and believed it, you are saved. You are born again in Christ. I want to encourage you to get connected with someone of faith and attend a church in your area where you can grow in the understanding of God. You can contact Eagle Worldwide Ministries in the United States and Canada, and we can help you find a church in your area. God bless you and your family.

IN THE MIDST OF THE BATTLE, THE LINES CAN SOMETIMES BECOME QUITE BLURRY. IN THIS MOMENT, MORE THAN EVER, WE NEED DISCERNMENT AND WISDOM FROM THE LORD, ALONG WITH THE SPIRIT OF MIGHT!

Revival

*I hear the voice of one calling, prepare ye the
way of the Lord,*
And make His paths straight in the wilderness.
And let your light shine in the darkness.
And let your rain fall in the desert.

As sure as gold is precious and the honey sweet,
So you love this city and you love these streets,
Every child out playing by their own front door,
Every baby lying on the bedroom floor.

Every dreamer dreaming in her dead-end job,
*Every driver driving through the rush hour
mob.*
I feel it in my spirit, feel it in my bones.
*You're going to send revival, bring them all
back home.*
I can hear that thunder in the distance.
Like a train on the edge of town.

Awaken to the Moment

I can feel the brooding of Your Spirit.
"Lay your burdens down, lay your burdens down."

From the preacher preaching when the well is dry,
To the lost soul reaching for a higher high.
From the young man working through his hopes and fears,
To the widow walking through the veil of tears.

Every man and woman, every old and young,
Every father's daughter, every mother's son.
I feel it in my spirit, feel it in my bones.
You're going to send revival, bring them all back home.

I can hear that thunder in the distance,
Like a train on the edge of town.
I can feel the brooding of Your Spirit.
"Lay your burdens down, lay your burdens down."

Revive us, revive us.
Revive us with Your fire![1]

1. Words and music by Robin Mark, copyright © Robin Mark/Elijah Music

JOIN US!

EAGLE WORLDWIDE WINTER AND SUMMER CAMP

Eagle Worldwide Ministries provides opportunities each year to fellowship, equip, and empower our Monthly Partners, Network Members, and all those hungry for the presence of the Lord. With guest speakers, nightly services, radical tabernacle worship, prophecy, signs and wonders, the Lord shows up in power in our midst!

Make plans to join Dr. Russ Moyer for one or both of our biannual camp meetings.

Summer Camp
July & August
Hamilton ON || Aurora ON

Winter Camp
January & February
Pensacola, FL

www.eagleworldwide.com // @EagleWorldwideMinistries

PERSONALIZED MENTORING!!

WITH DR. RUSS MOYER

Are you looking to take hold of everything God has for you in this moment and press into the destiny you were created for?

The Screaming Eagles personalized mentoring group is for you! Each group is customized to a particular topic from leadership and the prophetic to spiritual warfare. Dr. Russ takes practical life experiences from over 25 years in ministry and imparts to the next generation.

Email ashley@eagleworldwide.com for more details on how you can become a Screaming Eagle!

SCREAMING
EAGLES

EAGLE
WORLDWIDE MINISTRIES
■■■■■NETWORK

Credentialing
Spiritual Covering
Pastoral Support
Equipping
Networking

Find out how you can become a part of a family of ministers and ministries around the world having Kingdom impact!

As a five-fold ministerial network we value relationship, knowing those that labor among us, giving you the freedom to move and operate in the giftings God has placed in your life.

To find out if our Network is right for you, contact us using the information provided below.

(CAD)
P.O. BOX 39
COPETOWN ON L0R1J0
905.308.9991

(USA)
P.O. BOX 4357
PENSACOLA FL 32507
850.478.0895

www.eagleworldwidenetwork.com

PROPHETS WALKING TOGETHER IN UNITY TO DECLARE THE WORD OF THE LORD.

As the largest coalition of prophetic voices in North America, ICPL is an alliance where confirmed Prophets are able to relate to and connect with one another. We desire to be a safe environment for emerging prophetic voices to explore their gifting among seasoned leaders.

If you are a prophet, prophetic intercessor, or emerging prophetic voice, it is our desire that you would discover the valuable resources and relationships ICPL has to offer. You don't have to do ministry alone.

ICPL USA
P.O. BOX 4357 PENSACOLA FL, 32507
850.748.0895

ICPL CAN
P.O. BOX 39 COPETOWN ON, LOR 1J0
905.308.9991

(f) @ICPLeaders // www.ICPLeaders.com

NEED PRAYER?

Eagle Worldwide Ministries, People Who Pray, is an apostolic prayer network comprised of intercessors from around the globe, providing prayer covering for not just our Network of Ministers and Ministries, but for anyone who is in need!

Need prayer? Email Us! Our team of prayer warriors is ready to pray for you.

Interested in becoming a part of People Who Pray as one of our intercessors? Email us!

EMAIL US:

PEOPLEWHOPRAY@EAGLEWORLDWIDE.COM

ONLINE TRAINING!

EAGLE WORLDWIDE TRAINING CENTER

Equipping and Empowering you to fulfill your God given destiny!

CERTIFICATE PROGRAMS
MINISTERIAL DIPLOMAS
INDIVIDUAL COURSES

SCAN ME

WWW.EAGLEWORLDWIDETRAINING.COM

THE CENTRE FOR
EXCELLENCE
OF PENSACOLA

Impacting our community, one life at a time.

The Centre for Excellence is a US non-profit organization whose purpose is to offer practical resources, training, hope and support for individuals and families seeking to overcome a variety of life challenges including, but not limited to, poverty, addiction, and joblessness.

Visit the website below to see how you can join Dr. Russ in impacting lives by becoming a part of the Excellence Club today!

PROGRAMS & SERVICES

Food Distribution

Practical Skills Courses

Jamie's MOM'S HOUSE

Human Trafficking AWAREness

@Centre4Excellence.tdp

www.centre4excellence.com

Partner and Become a

KINGDOM ADVANCER
with Eagle Worldwide Ministries

Do you want to see people impacted with the life-changing power of the Gospel? Do you believe in the priesthood of the believer and that each one of us has a mandate to be fruitful, multiply, and demonstrate the power and gifts of the Holy Spirit?

If you answered yes, then we would like to invite you to partner with Eagle Worldwide Ministries. As you partner together with Dr. Russ and Pastor Mave Moyer and the Eagle Worldwide Team, your financial seed will bear much Kingdom fruit. Won't you become a Kingdom Advancer with us today?

Start your monthly giving today!
visit www.eagleworldwide.com/become-a-partner

Author Contact Page

You may contact the author in the following ways:

By Email
bro.russ @ eagleworldwide.com

By Phone:
⊦1 905 308 9991

By Mail:
PO Box 39
Copetown ON L0R1J0
Canada

On Facebook:

facebook.com/eagleworldwide

facebook.com/russ.moyer.52

By visiting his website:
www.EagleWorldwide.com

www.ingramcontent.com/pod-product-compliance
Lightning Source LLC
Chambersburg PA
CBHW032041090426
42744CB00004B/79